ENDORSEMENTS

If I was planning a motor home trip across the back roads of any country, I would want Pablo in that vehicle. He carries an infectious hope I witness in few others. He trims man-made moralism from the Bible's stories and reveals a God who adores us, knows us completely and deeply loves to communicate with us. This book is a courageous and very helpful guide for our own journeys, from one who makes no claims to be ahead of us. And so he is probably trusted more than most to guide us.

—JOHN LYNCH
Author of *On My Worst Day* and co-author of *The Cure*

In this book, Pablo takes you to the mountains and valleys, the rain forests and deserts of his life and walk with God. As you will see, it is God's desire to reclaim and release the profound and purposeful life that He has given you out of the world's artificial landscapes. God does this out of His intimate love for you and His understanding of who you are to be. Pablo's story will inspire and instruct you like few others do to take the same journey home.

—GARY BARKALOW
Best-selling author of *It's Your Call*

In a world that is searching for who they are and what they are called to do, *The Modern Fig Leaf: Uncovering your True Identity* is that book! Pablo opens the doors of Heaven to reveal the truth that has been buried inside of us since before time began! This book brings us to the "a-ha" moment we have been waiting for. I highly recommend this book!

—JEREMY LOPEZ
Founder of IdentityNetwork.net

Pablo captures in fresh words and dynamic images the ancient truths of our faith. We have lost the heart of the Gospel in our systems, structures, and institutions. Deeply rooted in Scripture, Pablo attempts to bring us home to the heart of the story—the heart of the Father—and in doing so brings us back home to our own heart. Put your feet up, sit back, and take a walk and talk with God to a place of peace, integrity, and total acceptance. You'll be surprised where you end up. I'll see you there.

—Mark Eaton
President, Eaton Leadership Foundation

Let the words of Pablo encourage your spirit on this sacred journey called life. We all need guides along the way. You will be greatly blessed by this sojourner who has marked the trail for those who follow.

—David L. Cook, PhD
Author of best-selling book *Golf's Sacred Journey*
Executive Producer of the motion picture *Seven Days in Utopia*

Professional coach and trainer Pablo Giacopelli has done it again. Maybe his best work yet. In this beautiful book, Pablo penetrates our inner world, reminding us that what we seek outside ourselves, God, or Dad, as Pablo reminds us to call Him, has provided already. We find ourselves, not by looking beyond but by looking within. Thanks again, Pablo, for helping us probe what's truly important— our inner life.

—Dr. Steve McSwain
Speaker, spiritual teacher, and author of the award-winning book
The Enoch Factor: The Sacred Art of Knowing God

the MODERN

FIG

LEAF

the MODERN
FIG
LEAF

UNCOVERING YOUR
TRUE IDENTITY

PABLO
GIACOPELLI

DESTINY IMAGE® PUBLISHERS, INC.

P.O. Box 310, Shippensburg, PA 17257-0310

"Promoting Inspired Lives."

This book and all other Destiny Image and Destiny Image Fiction books are available at Christian bookstores and distributors worldwide.

Cover design by: Christian Rafetto

For more information on foreign distributors, call 717-532-3040.

Reach us on the Internet: www.destinyimage.com.

ISBN 13 TP: 978-0-7684-0714-3

ISBN 13 eBook: 978-0-7684-0715-0

For Worldwide Distribution, Printed in the U.S.A.

1 2 3 4 5 6 7 8 / 19 18 17 16 15

DEDICATION

I would like to dedicate this book to the One who made my heart and chose to make His home inside it.

Because of You I am learning to remember who I truly am.

ACKNOWLEDGMENTS

If I am honest this is one part of every book I have written which I both love and hate at the same time. I love it because it reminds me of all the beautiful people Dad has sent my way to spur me on this journey I am on. In them I have seen Dad's invisible fingerprints as they have touched my life and led me to the next stage of my path. The hatred, if we can call it that, comes from knowing that I could not possibly thank everyone I would like for the obvious reasons.

Still I will have a good go and see where it takes us.

First and foremost I must begin by thanking my darling wife Madeleine. Your life has added so much to mine. I know that it is not always easy living with me; however, the sparks that sometimes fly are the evidence that we are alive and love each other enough to continue to work at this wonderful thing called our marriage. I love you today more than yesterday, and I am sure tomorrow it will be even more than today.

I would like to also thank my children: Vanessa, Jake, Mia, Gisella, and Anabella for often being my greatest teachers and friends. Thank you for your unconditional love and the simple way of seeing life that you have often helped me to see. My heart today is more alive and true because you guys have been and continue to be a part of my daily life. You rock and always remember that your dad loves you more than you will probably ever know.

Thank you to my friend, fellow ragamuffin, and board member Randy Shelley. This book would not have seen the light of day if it had not been for your commitment towards my life and your perseverance.

Thank you also to the rest of my board members Jeff Andrechyn, Darrell Amy, Rick Hartsell, Hunter Wright, Jeremy Lopez, and Jerry Lind. Your belief in me has and continues to make a world of difference.

Thank you to Ronda, Mykela, John, and the whole team at Destiny Image. Thank you for believing in me and the message I have been given. Your encouragement, hard work, and professionalism have made this journey a lot smoother than it could have been.

Thank you to Ryan Adair, my editor. Thank you for being so gentle with your "machete" and working so hard to keep the message intact when it could have been easier to change it.

Thank you to Jim Palmer for your friendship, coaching, insight, and your willingness to walk this part of the journey with me.

Thank you to Darin Hufford for his friendship, love, and commitment to my life and message.

To all those that though you did not get a mention your life and example have been a rich source of life and encouragement in everything I do and in who I am. I love you lots and I am eternally grateful for the part you have played and some of you continue to play in my life.

Last but certainly not least. Thank you to you my Eternal Dad. Is has all started with you and it will all finish with you. The in between is the fun I get to have as we both walk together hand in hand in this beautiful thing called my life.

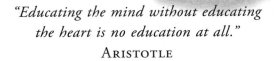

*"Educating the mind without educating
the heart is no education at all."*
ARISTOTLE

CONTENTS

Foreword 15

Introduction 17

PART I 21

Chapter 1   The Secret Within the Garden 23

Chapter 2   This Way or That Way? 33

Chapter 3   The Modern Fig Leaf 49

Chapter 4   Seeing the Truth. 67

PART II 85

Chapter 5   Inner Bleeding 87

Chapter 6   Breaking the Deal Up 105

Chapter 7   The Rest of Us 123

Chapter 8   Now. 143

Chapter 9   The Man in the Mirror. 159

Chapter 10   Our Biggest Allies 177

Chapter 11   It Was Never Meant to Last! 195

Chapter 12   Intimate Prayer. 215

Chapter 13   One 231

FOREWORD

It's late at night as you pull in to your driveway. Immediately you notice that you forgot to leave the porch light on. As you slowly approach your front door with key in hand, you can barely see a single thing in front of you. You reach out with your left hand, locating the doorknob, and then you use your pointer finger to find the keyhole. With your right hand, you guide the key to your finger and slip the house key in the hole. It goes in slightly and then stops. Why? The answer is frustratingly simple. The key is upside down.

This is precisely the predicament for a staggering number of sincere Christians across the globe. Because of the rigorous demands of trying to follow a performance-based religion, they find themselves approaching the Father in an upside-down fashion. They ultimately find that the key won't fit. It simply doesn't work that way.

The problem is that the things of the spirit appear upside down to the mind. Jesus bewildered the religious leaders of His day when He said things like "The first will be last and the last will be first" and "The greatest among you will be the servant of all," because it just didn't make sense to the natural mind. This is why they missed God when He stood right in front of them in the person of Jesus Christ.

In the following pages, Pablo Giacopelli describes in absolute clarity the predicament and the solution to upside-down thinking. I believe without question that this book is a game changer! It turns the key to the Kingdom right side up, showing the way to a real relationship with the Father.

—DARIN HUFFORD
Best-selling author of *The Misunderstood God*

INTRODUCTION

We come to the world naked, and we depart from it naked as well. So why do we try to cover our nakedness while living our daily lives? We create many fig leaves for our nakedness—how spiritual we are, how successful, our personal wealth—but for what? I don't know about you, but I want to stop pretending to be something I am not. I want to stop pretending to believe things I think or say when I really don't. I want to be real, raw, and uncensored before God, before those I come across, and to you.

Understanding this is what has led me to start living from a new reality I have found within my heart, thus changing my life. I am able to fully appreciate a sunset now. It is no longer rare to find myself crying about small things, which in the past I found insignificant and silly. I can see God and His expression in everyone and everything. Slowly but surely I catch myself loving what before I found difficult to even look at. When someone hurts me, I am learning not to hurt them back, but to take the time to try to understand why that person has chosen to act this way in the first place.

My persistent drive has led me to great heights of success as I found myself walking down the corridors where tennis history is made. I traveled the world, was driven around in expensive and luxurious cars, and when able, I enjoyed the lifestyle few ever have. Yet, with all of this, every time I looked at Jesus, I saw in Him something I didn't have. Yes, I had put my hand up and had prayed the prayer, but something was still missing. There was always a feeling like somewhere, somehow, a short circuit had taken place or a fuse had been burned out. I now realize that what caused this feeling was the disconnection that existed within me—not so much with my heart itself, but with the reality that resided within it.

Had you asked anyone, all would have told you I was a man of passion and grit. This was not the consequence of living life from the heart as much as it was an extreme striving to silence the wounds and pain I carried within, pain that disabled my ability to connect with the depths of my new heart. Much has happened since then, and much has been discovered since I accepted the invitation handed to me some years back. I am glad I chose to travel down this track and away from the one I was on.

It is easy to read something and then criticize others, and for this reason I have started with the man in the mirror. If we all take the step of reconnecting to the God-reality that resides within our hearts and trust that our new hearts are good, then the vine will be more full of fruit and much healthier. Our focus will then be on that dimension where we discover how we are loved and not on trying to always manage and fix our behavior. I believe Dad[1] longs for this too, and so it is with this sentiment I present to you this humble offering.

As you read, you will be a witness of what my path has looked like as I have pursued living from my heart, not at the expense of my mind or humanity but fully integrated with both of these. I have divided this book into two parts. Part I will help us build a foundation to show why the heart is so important and what we are missing if we don't engage with it in our lives. Part II will be a vulnerable and true account of what it looks like in my life to live out of this new reality.

You will notice that at the end of each chapter, I have included a prayer and a point of action; you can elect to undertake one, both, or neither of them. They are simple and were written with you in mind. Their intended purpose is to help you encapsulate and practically express what perhaps will be difficult to do after you read each chapter. I sincerely hope you take the time to incorporate these small suggestions into your daily life, because I am only too aware of the huge difference one sees in their journey when becoming involved and immersed in it.

It is, therefore, my sincerest hope and prayer that, as you turn the pages of this book and share with me the journey I am taking (for it is far from done), you begin to see your own journey enhanced and brought to a new place, where life will be less about becoming and more about enjoying what you already are and have always been.

I now realize that grace is leading me into a place where I am able to suddenly give to others what they are not able to give me. The reality is that I could go on because of the impact this way of approaching life has had upon me. However, it is now important that you have a chance to see the way this has all been happening in my life. I invite you to join me in this journey.

Travel well, my friend.

PABLO

NOTE

1. As you read this edition of my journey, you will find that I no longer call God Father or Lord, but Dad. This new way of expressing my understanding of Him is nothing more than a ragamuffin who has found someone he can trust, much like a child trusts his dad.

PART I

CHAPTER 1

THE SECRET WITHIN THE GARDEN

God, you were here all along and I never knew it.
—JACOB

You've gone a million miles
How far'd you get
To that place where you can't remember
And you can't forget
—BRUCE SPRINGSTEEN

An episode of one of my favorite programs on the Discovery Channel is coming to an end, and I see out of the corner of my eye my little girl, Gisella, hiding behind the couch. "It must be her bedtime," I think. My thought is quickly confirmed when I hear my wife shout in the distance, "Pabloooooo. Gisella needs to go to bed."

I pick my gaze back up and smile as my eyes lock with Gisella's, and she motions for me to be quiet by putting her little finger over her mouth and whispering "shhhhh." Believe it or not, I have grown to love these evening cabarets in which she somehow thinks no one is going to notice her hiding behind the couch. I can't help but admire her tenacity, as night after night she fights a battle she will undoubtedly never win. Like her, I can't help myself each time either—much to my wife's dismay.

Eventually, as my wife begins to lose her voice from reminding us that we are breaking the house rules, Gisella and I comply, and we walk hand in hand into her room. This night is like any other night. We pray together, play around, and say good night to the two Minnie Mouse dolls that share the bed. I usually lie down next to her, waiting for her little eyelids to finally lose the battle to stay awake. On this particular night, as I lie there, I once again begin to think about my heart and how far it has come in the last few years as I have learned to loosen the grip around my life.

After some time, I turn my head over to check on Gisella and see that she is by now fast asleep. As I begin to get up from her bed, I suddenly hear Dad whisper as clear as day into my heart, "The Garden of Eden is a picture of your heart."

This stops me completely in my tracks. "What was that about?" I think as I quietly and slowly continue to work my way out of her room. Closing the door behind me and heading into the living room, my wife asks, "Is she asleep?" I nod my head in confirmation.

The next morning I can't shift my thoughts away from what I heard last night. As I lie in bed, I realize Dad wants to show me something new about my heart that perhaps will answer the questions I have been asking. One of those questions has been, "When, what, where, and how did all this go so wrong, causing us to believe that living life from the heart is so foolish and unwise?"

I quickly turn on my iPad and open my Bible app. I search for Genesis 1, and when I find it, I ask, "Dad, what are You trying to show me by telling me that the Garden of Eden is a picture of my heart?"

As I begin to read the Bible, I realize that the Garden of Eden is an actual place that can be found in the Middle East. Its exact location, like everything else in institutionalized religion, has been debated over the years. Yet it is safe to say that it is a real place and it can be found somewhere in the Middle East. "If it's a real place," I ask myself, "then how can it be a picture of our heart?"

Some minutes go by, and once again I hear Dad as He whispers into my heart, "I am going to help you understand what really happened in the Garden, which will then help you see why it is that so many choose not to live their lives out of the reality that is within their hearts."

Several days go by without any further revelation about the Garden or what I heard back in Gisella's room. I find myself boarding a plane one evening for a transatlantic flight that will keep me in the air for more than 12 hours. After I board the plane, I find my seat and expectantly wait for the boarding process to come to an end to see if someone will sit next to me. Much to my surprise, I am the only one in my section without a fellow passenger in the next seat.

As the door on the plane is closed, I smile as I think how well I am going to sleep. A few minutes into the flight, however, I once again open my Bible app and turn my attention to Genesis 1. I begin to read about the Garden of Eden once again.

Suddenly, Dad whispers, "The way I lived and related with Adam and Eve within the Garden is the way I long to relate with you within your heart. The Garden of Eden is a picture where you can see the reason why it is that you and everyone else find it so difficult to relate with Me. You see, Pablo, what I want you to understand is what really happened in that Garden all those years ago and how this still affects the reality you and everyone else are born into."

I sit there. I am not exactly sure what He means, although I can clearly see that this is going to take more than one conversation to understand. It becomes obvious that I am about to be taken on an awesome journey where much of what I will be discovering will enable me to bring many things I have learned along the way into a full circle of understanding.

"Take a look at Genesis 1:26 and tell me what you see," Dad says. I find the Scripture and silently read: "God spoke: 'Let us make human beings in our image, make them reflecting our nature....'" I read it several times before I lower my iPad and look out the window into the dark night.

The moon is shining in all its glory, lighting up the ocean beneath us. The air outside looks smooth, and so my thoughts are captured as I see all of this and meditate on what I have just read and have been hearing. I sit with the mixture of feeling blessed and amazed at how far I have come where I can actually converse with God as I am doing this evening at 38,000 feet. This has not always been the case. It has been a long process, much the same way a newborn baby learns to recognize the voice of his or her parents. There has been much trial and error, but as I have continued to walk this journey out from my heart, this still small voice has become clearer.

As I direct my eyes back to the iPad and look at the same verse again, I realize that even though I have read it many times before, I finally see something tonight I have never seen before. For the first time I begin to enter into the full reality of my real and original identity. I realize that within me, inside my heart, I am one with Dad.

As I am enjoying this moment of discovery, something comes to mind that says, "So you really think you and God are one?" The thought is accompanied by a distinct feeling of fear, which suggests I am elevating myself to the same level as God—that what I am feeling, in other words, is that I am like God.

No sooner have I begun to entertain this thought then Dad interrupts me: "This is exactly where the problem begins. Like Adam and Eve, you don't really understand your true identity. The enemy knows that as long as he can keep you away from understanding who you truly are, then you will continue to work really hard all of your life to somehow reach the same reality of the Garden. Yet all along, even though you don't realize it, what you are trying to reach outside is already within you."

He continues by saying, "If you remember when the enemy met Jesus in the desert, the one thing he tried so hard was to challenge His identity." As I hear this, I quickly turn to the Gospels to look again at the passage of Jesus's temptation, which closely parallels the temptation of Adam and Eve.

The devil says to Jesus, "Since You are God's Son, speak the word that will turn these stones into loaves of bread" (Matthew 4:3). I see that this statement is incredibly similar to the one he makes to Eve in Genesis 3:4-5: "God knows that the moment you eat from the tree, you'll see what's really going on. You'll be just like God."

Wait a minute. Did he just say, "You *will* be"? Genesis 1:26 clearly states that we are made in Dad's image and have His nature—present tense. So what exactly are we missing before we can be like God?

What Satan is clearly trying to do is plant the same seed of doubt in Jesus he planted in Eve when he challenged her and Adam's identity. Adam and Eve, unlike Jesus, acted on it by biting into the fruit of the tree God had advised Adam not to eat from. Jesus, on the other hand, didn't do what the enemy suggested. He knew the truth and understood that this action would only lead Him into the same place Adam and Eve got themselves into.

"It is so clear. Why didn't I see this before?" I think to myself.

I understand now how Adam and Eve thought that Dad had somehow shortchanged them and left something out of them when He created them. Yet again, Genesis 1:26 reveals nothing was further from the truth. This is why Jesus does not bother to answer the enemy's attempt by choosing not to do what he is challenging Him to do, which is to prove that He is indeed the Son of God.

This is clear as we see again how Jesus answers the devil by pointing out the truth from Deuteronomy: "It takes more than bread to stay alive. It takes a steady stream of words from God's mouth" (Matthew 4:4). Jesus knew very well who the source of His life was and whose identity He carried within.

I notice the same attempt by the enemy to plant doubt in Jesus about who He is as he begins the next challenge: "Since You are God's Son, jump" (Matthew 4:5). The interesting thing here is that the enemy also tries to put in doubt Dad's identity and nature, as he did in the Garden, when he quotes Psalm 91.

I suddenly see why the enemy works so hard to blind us to the true identity and nature of God. He realizes that, at the same time he does this, he is also blinding us to who we really are. This helps me understand how flawed an approach it is when all we try to do is discover who God is without paying one bit of attention to discovering who we truly are.

When we discover who we truly are, we discover who Dad truly is. This is why Jesus again counters the enemy by ignoring his attempt to try to negotiate Him away from His true identity and Dad's true nature. He does this by declaring the truth: "Don't you dare test the Lord your God" (Matthew 4:7).

"Wow! How did I miss this?" I ask myself. "I mean, I have always seen this as a test Jesus had to pass in order to be ready to begin His ministry and to set a standard for all of us to follow every time we are tested."

Suddenly, Dad whispers, "Pablo, this is what happens when you read the Bible through the eyes of your false self. You see everything as a performance and a prescription, a task that needs to be accomplished and a goal that needs to be reached. In the process you miss the truth that is within you and hidden behind the words that have been written. Always remember that Scripture is like a manhole cover that can only be opened from your heart, so you can discover the real sentiment I had within My heart when I inspired the Scriptures to be written."

After hearing this, I turn my attention to the rest of the passage in front of me by reading Matthew 4:8-9, where, once again, the enemy—through a clever turn of words—attempts to rob Jesus of His identity by inviting Him to worship him in exchange for what is not his to give. Jesus again declares the truth and tells the enemy to beat it, as He bluntly shows him that He is fully aware of His true identity and His Dad's nature. These two things are not up for negotiation as far as He is concerned.

As I turn my attention to the beautiful evening outside the plane, I once again realize that, unfortunately, this was not the case all those years ago in the Garden—nor is it the case with many of us today.

I continue to sit dumbfounded by what I am just beginning to understand. I realize that, essentially, in the Garden, Dad gave us His spiritual DNA when He made each one of us. Nothing can change this. Nothing—absolutely nothing—not even what we do or don't do, say or don't say, pray or don't pray, decide or don't decide. This, my dear friends, is the fundamental truth of who we are within our hearts. This is our true Self, where we are fused together with Dad. We are one with Him; we have His nature and His image placed within us. Each one of us carries this reality within, whether we have prayed a prayer of repentance or not.

"If this is the truth, how come so many of us can't see it?" I ask Dad. "In fact, where exactly are we living from when we don't live from this place?"

I hear Him whisper with—I bet with a million bucks—a smile on His face, "Let me show you."

I turn to Genesis 2:16-17, where Dad tells Adam, not Eve, "You can eat from any tree in the garden, except from the Tree-of-Knowledge-of-Good-and-Evil. Don't eat from it. The moment you eat from that tree, you're dead."

I read this and immediately see the word "dead" at the end of the verse, which I have never focused on before. "Why did You say that Adam would be dead if he ate from this tree? Clearly, after he and Eve ate, they didn't die?"

"Pablo, you are still looking at things on the surface," Dad responds. "You thought that when I told Adam he would die, it meant that he would physically die. You have seen it this way all along because you have seen it with the eyes of your flesh and not with the eyes of your heart."

There my eyes are opened, and I realize that what Dad meant was that they would spiritually die immediately and physically die eventually, which Adam did when he reached the old age of nine hundred and thirty.

"If they died spiritually that day, then from where did they start living and what happened to their hearts?" I ask. I hear nothing more. The silence tells me that the answer to this question is for another time. I have clearly heard what I needed to hear for this moment. Yes, the thoughts continue to fumble in my mind as I try to figure it out. No matter how hard I try, however, nothing makes sense apart from what I have just discovered. As I lean back in my seat, I am beginning to get tired, and soon I close my eyes and fall asleep for the remainder of the flight.

What follows is a long period of time where Dad takes me on an incredible journey, where He begins to show me the roles our heart and spirit play in our lives, and why and how the enemy tries to take us out from being able to live from them. I will go on to discover what these two are replaced by and how this divides and causes us to live under an illusion instead of in the truth that is responsible for setting and keeping us free.

One thing I realize now is that by the end of that night, inside that plane, somewhere over the Atlantic, I had begun to catch a glimpse of the truth that would revolutionize my life in the days ahead. I would begin to understand and see that all that had taken place within the Garden of Eden was exactly what takes place in all of our lives today from the moment we are born. Despite this new understanding, nothing could have prepared me for what Dad would show me next.

PRAYER

God, thank You for this opportunity You are giving me once again to discover who I really am. You know the condition of my life and how I am reaching this part of my journey. To be honest, it scares me a bit. I know what I have heard before about the heart. Yet for some reason, I want to read more. You know that down deep I long for You and want to somehow reach that place where I understand what this is all about, that space where I can understand who You really are and who I really am, where I can finally feel loved and at peace in my entire being and not just when I get it right.

I am tired of listening to others tell me what You like, love, and want. I want to find this out for myself. So, God, I am going to take a chance and give this book a go. All I ask from You is that You would help me lay down all my good ideas and arguments long enough that I may somehow be able to see what You are trying to show me as I read. Amen.

POINT OF ACTION

God loves gardens. In Eden it was "our will be done," and in Gethsemane it was "Your will be done." Take some time to meditate these next few days to see what it might look like in your daily routine to share the garden of your life with God. I encourage you to write your discoveries down and add to them as revelation is given to you.

CHAPTER 2

THIS WAY OR THAT WAY?

You can eat from any tree in the garden, except
from the Tree-of-Knowledge-of-Good-and-Evil
—GOD

Love saves. Love heals. Love motivates.
Love unites. Love returns us to our origins,
as here lies the ultimate act of saving,
of healing, of overcoming dualism.
—ANONYMOUS

Welcome to Denver International Airport, sir. How can I help you today?" an attendant asks me as I approach the baggage claim area. "I must once again look like I am lost," I think as I smile and thank her, letting her know I think I know where I am going. I have come to visit a long-time friend and mentor of mine with whom I have been working for several years, yet I have never had the chance to give him a hug in person. I finally find my bags and see what looks like my friend over in the distance. He waves for me to wait for him, because he is on an important call with a business contact. I hesitantly oblige because

I have been sitting on my butt now for more than 18 hours. Anyhow, I sit down and wait for him.

As I spend the next few days with my friend, I find myself battling jet lag and locked in a conversation with him. "You know, Dad has been speaking to me about the Garden of Eden and our new heart. Something happened in the Garden that caused us to see things differently. You know what I mean?"

I continue, "You know how there are two trees there? And of one of them, Dad speaks and tells Adam not to eat from it, whereas he can from all the others." I pause a moment. "The thing is that I see much of what is going on in the Garden to be like a code that needs to be deciphered. For example, what do the tree of the knowledge of good and evil and the tree of life represent?" I ask my mentor. In a way I also put the question out there for Dad to use this opportunity to show me something about my heart, my true identity, and the Garden.

We talk some more and he says, "Pablo, you know, in my view, the tree of the knowledge of good and evil is the law—right and wrong, good and bad, black and white." As these words leave his mouth, I know I am in a moment of revelation. Our conversation continues, and we touch on other areas of the heart and life. At the end of it, however, I know this is where I must focus my attention next.

During the next few days, I spend much time on my own because my friend is busy with work. This gives me a great opportunity to be alone with Dad and to ask some much-needed questions. "So, Dad," I say with a smile, "something happened in the Garden by that tree where Adam and Eve bit into that apple, didn't it?" I ask. "I am guessing it had something to do with the way all of us choose to approach—at one stage or another—our lives as well as the reality we are born into."

I open my Bible app and start to read the book of Genesis once again. My focus is turned to Genesis 3, where the enemy begins his conversation with a suggestive question by asking, "Do I understand that God told you not to eat from *any* tree in the garden?" (Genesis 3:1).

The enemy is trying to suggest to Eve that Dad is somehow holding something back from her and Adam. The reality Adam and Eve were living in was unified and whole. There was perfect harmony, and the perception of separation was not present. There was no duality, no right and wrong, no good or evil, no black or white—there was no life or death. There was only one reality— the truth. Adam and Eve were fully integrated and functioning from both their divine and human natures without there being any conflict between the two.

Eve's reply to the serpent shows us that there isn't any other reality she doesn't know or see: "Not at all. We can eat from the trees in the garden. It's only about the tree in the middle of the garden that God said, 'Don't eat from it; don't even touch it or you'll die'" (Genesis 3:3-4). This tree was not to one side or the other in the Garden, but it was right in the middle of it. Dad had clearly not hidden this tree, which meant that it was not only an important tree but also a tree on which much hinged.

Furthermore, if the Garden of Eden is a picture of the human heart, then this means the law and the truth are, therefore, both found within our new heart. This is why Jesus said in Matthew 5:17, "Do not think that I came to abolish the Law or the Prophets; I did not come to abolish but to fulfill" (NASB). He is basically saying that He had come to fulfill the law as a human being, and this could be done as long as a person lived out of the truth within his or her heart.

The same thing was happening with Adam and Eve until they decided to take matters into their own hands. Up until this point, Adam and Eve were living in a reality where there was absolutely no separation in their eyes. Their lives were whole and undivided. Life flowed from the heart, where they were one with Dad. They didn't know anything else but oneness with Dad.

We then see the enemy's tactics to disconnect us from this unified reality as he leads Eve to purchase the first illusion he has sold to humanity, and which has since then become a reality we work hard to keep going (see Genesis 3:4-5). The serpent knows that if he can get Eve and Adam to bite into the fruit of the tree in the middle of the Garden, then he will cause their spirits to die, just like Dad said they would.

It is important to remember that the heart is the wellspring of life and where all life begins.[1] We clearly see this even today when the first ultrasound image of a child shows him inside his mother's womb—even before one can see the brain fully formed. It is also possible to hear and even sometimes see a heartbeat in those images. Over the years, I have come to see our spirit as the radar that scans everything around us, even the invisible realm, and then relates that information back to the heart where we understand it. This often happens without us even knowing how to describe or label it.

It is important also to remember that Dad is a Spirit, and we are spirits occupying a body, and not the other way around. Therefore, if we take all of this into consideration, it is easy to understand how in the minute our spirits die, we become handicapped by losing our ability to be aware of the spiritual reality in and around our life as a whole. This is the main reason why we become disconnected from the reality of the Garden within our heart. And this is why Dad announced that alongside our new heart, we would also be given a new spirit.[2]

Eve is no longer looking at things from her heart. She is now using her mind to see things as she focuses on what the apple looks like, as well as what she will or won't get out of it, instead of living from her heart, remaining within the reality where she is complete, whole, and lacking no good thing. (See Genesis 3:6.)

Now I understand why Dad made a point to tell Adam to guard and keep the Garden, as we are also told in Proverbs 4:23 to guard our hearts. Yet, like Adam, if we are honest many of us ignore our hearts preferring to focus on managing what we choose to think inside our minds. Adam was responsible for the condition of the garden as we are for the condition of our hearts. Dad's command to him was clear when he used the word *Uleshamra*, which means not to let anything compromise or violate what has been entrusted into our care. In his case, this included Eve as she was given to him once he had been placed in there.

Do you take care of your heart in this way?

I know I didn't for years and clearly neither did Adam. Like him we all suffer the consequences of this neglect. In his case we see that it was him who allowed, as we do, the enemy to violate the garden grounds and successfully disconnect him from the reality he and Eve enjoyed prior to the fall. Adam failed as a protector of himself and as a keeper of the Garden and his and Eve's hearts. This is why eight times we are told in the New Testament that sin entered the world through him and not her. This failure meant that he became the greatest loss in creation, and this is why Jesus had to come as a man.

Furthermore, Adam's reaction, when trying to find a reason why his life suddenly seemed out of sync, was to accuse Dad and blame him for selling him out in his choice of companion.

You can't help but realize what happened then is the same thing that is at work in us each time we look to blame others for our shortcomings. Yet all along it is simply the consequence of neglecting to live out of and care for the garden within our hearts. Remember, it is impossible to care for a garden unless you are inside it.

The minute Eve takes a bite from the apple, the eyes of her mind are opened and she begins to see things under the illusion of separation. Adam and Eve notice they are naked and not clothed, and their sense of awareness begins to come from their bodies, whereas before their awareness came through their spirits.

The separation spills over to their view of Dad. (See Genesis 3:8.) It is important to remember that up until this point, there is no mention of Dad and them being separated or disconnected from one another. In fact, they have been in the Garden for some time and not once have they tried or needed to hide from Him until now.

It is also important to bear in mind that before all of this happens, not once is there any mention that they have lost their true identity. However, all that has changed because now they are under an illusion, due to their spirits being dead, that they have become disconnected from their true identity.

Their focus is now completely fixed on what is outside of them. This new illusion they have come into has suddenly stripped away all true identity, purpose, meaning, love, joy, peace, happiness, acceptance, wisdom, understanding, health, hope, faith, value, worth, security, protection, grace, and peace. This nakedness they feel is the first clue we are given that neither their bodies nor their minds were ever designed to give them what their hearts can and did up until that point.

What happened through this moment is that Adam and Eve began to function from their minds and ceased to operate from their hearts. They began to look at things as if they were separated from God, which means they saw and perceived things differently than they did before. In the process, they lost sight of their true identity and the reality they had been living in up until that point—living in wholeness, free from shame or any other reality than that of oneness with Dad. Adam and Eve became dead to their true identity and forgot about it as they became disconnected from it.

We need to see that our lives have an underlying premise that is required for all of us to function in the way we were always meant to function. Adam and Eve had everything they needed for wholeness within them in the Garden, while they were living out of their hearts, where the very image and nature of God provided these for them. Now that they are seeing things with their minds, they have started to try to find things outside of themselves to make them whole. By now, the enemy has successfully managed to blind and disconnect them from their true identity found inside their hearts where they are still made in the image and nature of God.

Their minds tell them they need to start working hard to get what they lack—to be like God—through what they do and what they manage to become. This is the reason why Dad was telling them not to eat from the tree in the middle of the Garden in the first place—He was essentially telling them they would be bringing rules into their relationship with Him.

The moment we choose to live out of our mind alone, we will spend the rest of our days serving the rules because we will think that doing so will get back all those basic premises only God can give. All the rules will do, however, is control us and what we do with our lives. They will make it all become about our will and our ego, and how we can somehow fix things and make them right once again.

As we do this, however, we will always be given the sense that we are found wanting. This will lead us to toil in order to create a new identity that we will use to cover the shame we feel from being disconnected from our true identity found within our heart. Worse yet, we will use these rules to control one another, as we tell ourselves that we have been found wanting every time we miss the mark, which then leads us to toil even harder.

Living outside of our hearts, we will have to toil because doing what we love will become much harder. We will often be forced to do whatever it takes just to survive. The trust and grace our relationship was grounded in, where us and Dad were completely open and honest with each other, will disappear and we will be led to think that we are somehow uninvolved, displeasing, distant, and separated from Him because we are not able to meet the demands of the law.

Furthermore, these rules will bring us into a reality where division will be the foundation of our lives. This will lead us to divide our being by separating our humanity from our divinity, and we will erroneously try to sacrifice one to please the other. Yet, while we are busy doing all of this, we will only be helping to destroy our lives further, as we know that a home divided against itself will not stand. We will lose the balance that our integrated life gave us as it flowed from our heart. Shame and fear will be our new energy sources.

We will no longer focus on what is within us because we will be too busy trying to get it right and making things look better on the outside. We will fall under the illusion that the more we add to our life, the more likely we will be to reach the happiness and peace we need. We will hurt and even kill others in our quest for this happiness and peace, but we will never find it outside of ourselves.

The happiness and peace we seek has been within us all along, within our true Self, where we are still one with Dad. But, unfortunately, we will be blind to it as long as our mind and body continue to try to find it through satisfying our man-made rules.

"Do you want your life to be this way, Pablo?" Dad asks me as I finish writing the previous paragraph in my notes.

"No, Dad. I don't. And I don't think any one of us does," I reply.

"You are right," He says. "However, many can't see this and that's because they are trying to work it out in their minds by building theologies and man-made formulas that will somehow give them the illusion that they understand me and have figured me out. All these will do is divide them instead of bringing clarity and unity through their spirit and their hearts. For them it is about who is right and wrong and who owns the truth. This leads people to box others into a particular way of doing things instead of realizing that I have made everyone different and, therefore, I long to relate with everyone in a different way."

After hearing this, I lie back in my chair and catch a glance at the clock in the kitchen, realizing that I have been here for several hours. I decide to get up and stretch a bit. While stretching, my thoughts are taken back a few days to when I was standing at the airport waiting to pick up my baggage. I think to myself, "How much baggage I must have picked up along the way, as I tried to satisfy the law that has only added the weight and obstacles that have kept me disconnected from my true Self."

My time comes to an end in Denver. I say goodbye to my friend and mentor, and I walk into the airport to catch my flight. As I enter the terminal, Dad whispers into my heart, "The way is narrow and a few find it."

"Yeah, I know that," I reply.

To which He replies, "Yes, you know it, but you don't really understand it."

I smile as I sense that this has to do with what I have just discovered during my brief stay in Denver. "Okay, Dad. Let me check in, and then we can talk about it," I say with a smile that comes from the excitement within me.

I check in and fumble my three carry-ons toward the TSA security checkpoint. I realize I have too much carry-on luggage, so I will probably have trouble boarding the plane. I have been here before and, admittedly, I am not proud of it, but after traveling for many years I have developed a skill that usually enables me to get through the final boarding area without my bags being noticed.

But still, these bags are heavy, and they are an absolute pain. This is why, eventually, making it to my gate makes me happy. I notice that boarding is starting any minute now.

I put my bags down and sit for a quick rest, when I feel Dad asking me, "It is hard to stay in balance when you carry so much, isn't it?" He continues, "I want to show you something when you get inside the plane." As I hear this, the announcement to board begins.

My seating zone is the first to board. I get up and approach the counter, and, somehow again, I manage to get by the lady who is very busy conversing with her colleague while she checks people through.

As I enter the wide jetway, I relax my hold on the bags. I realize it is wide, and I have enough space for my bags and me—plus, no one is watching me. This, however, changes drastically after I get inside the plane. Without exception, the aisles on every plane I have flown in are narrow, which means that with every step you take, you bump into something or someone. Today is no different.

Dad reminds me of what He whispered to me earlier as I entered the airport. I finally reach my seat. After I take up most of the bin space above me with my bags, Dad shows me how the bags that just caused me to stumble, fall, and lose my balance on this narrow aisle represent all the knowledge, masks, labels, conditions, and wounds I continually carry with me.

He shows me these are the things that tell me if I carry them, I will have the necessary proof to calm my insecure faith and shame and show that I am walking on the narrow way Jesus spoke about. He shows me how my dualistic mind is causing me to think and see this way. That's why the road I find myself on is often the wide one, making entering and even remaining on the narrow road—with all the baggage I am carrying—impossible.

My immediate reaction is that I need to change the baggage I am carrying for something different. To which Dad suggests, "How about you just drop it all and travel lightly as Jesus encouraged His disciples to do?"

I finally understand. When we travel with a lot of baggage, our attention and focus is mostly on carrying and taking care of our baggage. The last thing we notice is whether we are on the right path or not. As long as we are walking and moving, we think that we must be on the right path. But nothing could be further from the truth.

We can all agree that traveling with fully laden bags—which affect our balance—doesn't just distract us, but it prevents us from enjoying and noticing the walk and anyone else who might be walking with us. Unfortunately, our religious bags are many and heavy. There is no room for both our luggage and ourselves on the narrow way. All the arguments, knowledge, labels, theologies, safety devices, good intentions, false pretenses, and wounding that are contained within them only add weight to our lives. These unnecessary extras will always lead us to the wide and spacious way that Jesus said would lead to destruction, because this is the only path it can all fit on.

On the narrow road, there is only room for us—no baggage allowed. This is all we need to carry with us because within we already have everything we need to be happy, at peace, and in balance. Our enlightenment begins when we start to loosen our grip around our religious bags. We can then return to that place within us where we are whole. These bags need to be seen as an anchor that keeps us bound to them through what we do or don't do. We need to understand that on the narrow road, it is grace and truth that keeps us there and not our own effort, hard work, or the extras we carry with us.

During this day, I finally begin to understand that when we awaken to the truth that sets us free, it does not mean that we add or replace our knowledge, conditions, arguments, self-imposed rules, and theologies we carry in our mind. But instead, we completely shed them. Jesus said that He had not come to abolish the law, but to fulfill it. Adam and Eve were fulfilling the law without even knowing it when they lived from their hearts.

The only way to find the narrow way is through grace and truth, and that is the only way to remain on it as well. The law leads us in one way or another, which causes our heart to be absent. It is impossible to abide in our heart fully while trying to fulfill the law. The law is either right or wrong, good or bad, black or white, in or out, accepted or rejected, love or fear, compassion or hate, heaven or hell. There is no in-between and no one reality, balance, or wholeness.

I am reminded of Jesus's words when He commanded His listeners to be whole like their Father in heaven was whole. (See Matthew 5:48.) Every time Jesus was asked about the Kingdom, He told His listeners that the Kingdom of heaven was right here, right now, and it was within them. Jesus always pointed people into themselves because He knew the truth that would set them free would be found in the truth of the Kingdom reality that was within them—and not in what they found outside of themselves.

Jesus knew that the sight of the same identity, which had been lost all those years back in the Garden, was still within each and every one of us. That place—where we are fused together with Dad and are made in His image and have His nature—was still there, it was just covered up because of the separation we thought we were now experiencing with Dad.

It is true that we are all born sinners—I am in no way denying that. However, we are not born sinners because we are dirty, disgusting, and Dad is separated from us and finds us repulsive. The real reason why we are sinners is because we are born into a reality that falls short of who we really are—from living in the wholeness Adam and Eve lived in before the fall. We are not the problem, but the reality we are born into, which we are also responsible for perpetuating, is the problem. And sin is the by-product of attempting to do life in this secondary reality with parts of us, our mind and body, which were never created for this central purpose.

This is why Jesus got upset with those who didn't admit they were sinners and He was attracted to those who were happy to admit it. Jesus never spoke about perfect behavior. Instead, He pointed us toward the perfection that was already within our true Self. He understood we had no chance of making it in the way we were going, and that is why it was necessary for Him to break this cycle.

Jesus said, "It is finished," at the cross as He too came under this illusion of separation but did not submit or live by it. Jesus was the perfect sacrifice fully able to reconnect us to our true identity that Adam and Eve disconnected themselves from in the Garden. Through His blood, Jesus cleansed the sin that is responsible for blinding and keeping us separated from the reality that is within us, so that we can also live a life that is in this world but not of it.

We need to wake up and understand that Dad has been with us since the beginning of our days—all the way back to that day when He knitted us together within our mothers' wombs, and even before. This is the grace that has sustained us all along. Anyone who genuinely believes that Dad has been watching them from a distance until they prayed a prayer, has not understood grace or the God behind it.

He loved us first and always so we could have a chance to love Him again. This is our Dad, who—although we didn't see Him or acknowledge Him—has been fathering us all along. The day we wake up, we don't see something new that wasn't there before. It's only that we suddenly are able to see what has been there all along.

As my plane lands at my next stop, I can't see much out of the window, because it is very late at night. I have been traveling all day, and again this revelation has brought more questions with it. As I deplane, I am conscious and aware that this way of living has meant I have spent much time and effort trying to cover the shame that this illusion of separation and right and wrong has brought into my life.

The question I was really asking now was, "If Adam and Eve covered their shame and themselves with a fig leaf, what else had I been using, apart from my good intentions, to cover myself?"

PRAYER

God, please help me see every time I try to get it right in order to please the law instead of relating with You. Help me to see the ways in which I have focused my life on the systems I have built around me, which give me a false sense of security. I realize that letting go of these is going to be hard. Please give me the ability to trust that You are walking with me, that I will indeed find everything I need when I let go of these heavy bags I have been carrying for so long. Please help me to understand Your grace in a whole new way, so I can see that I am going to trip up many times before I can understand what it means to travel light and trust You. You know how much I want to suddenly understand this wholeness that is within me, where You and I are one, and where I am made in Your image and have Your nature.

POINT OF ACTION

Write down some thoughts about what it might look like to approach certain situations in your life with an open, expectant, and neutral approach instead of the either/or mentality you have been using until now.

NOTES

1. See Proverbs 4:23, where we are told, "Keep vigilant watch over your heart; that's where life starts."

2. In Ezekiel 36:26 God says, "I'll give you a new heart, *put a new spirit in you.*"

CHAPTER 3

THE MODERN FIG LEAF

Looks aren't everything. Don't be impressed with his looks and stature. I've already eliminated him. God judges persons differently than humans do. Men and women look at the face; God looks into the heart.
—GOD

Humans are satisfied with whatever looks good; God probes for what is good.
—KING SOLOMON

Labels are for cans, not people.
—ANTHONY RAPP

B y now you have probably gathered that I am someone who aims to live from my heart. Because this walk of ours is a lifelong journey, it is one that requires much practice and being present. Like many today, I too lived my life absent and away from what was really happening. I sought to manipulate the world I lived in and the people I shared it with. And I did all of this in the name of results because these, unfortunately, have become the vectors we all look at when trying to figure out who a person, entity, or even our own self is.

I have now arrived at my next destination where I will be sharing with a new community of people for the next few days. As much as I would like to, I am unable to smoke inside the apartment I am staying at during my short visit, so I decide to wrap up and step outside where I open a cold beer and light my cigar. As I take a seat on the cushioned chair, I am met by a fresh and still night, embraced by a dark canvas of pure artistry. Tonight Dad desires to continue our conversation about the Garden of Eden and my new heart.

I have come a long way since that evening in my daughter's bedroom. Even though a lot has been revealed, the revelation about the practical stuff I always want to understand has just begun. My focus is now firmly fixed on that fig leaf Adam and Eve used to cover themselves once they bought in to the illusion of separation. I need one more layer on because it is so cold outside, so I go back in to grab a coat. As I put it on, I suddenly realize that this leaf had nothing to do with the elements I was trying to protect myself from.

This becomes more obvious as we see Dad killing two animals to clothe Adam and Eve just before they step out of the Garden. Clearly, this new way of seeing things has brought in a new dimension that required Adam and Eve to cover up for another reason that had nothing to do with the elements that affect all of us.

"They had forgotten their true identity, Pablo," Dad suddenly speaks into my heart. "When you forget who you are, you have to find your identity in something or someone else, other than who you truly are. They didn't know who they were anymore. Apart from Me, they were unable to see their true identity."

As Dad whispers this into my heart, the Scripture—where Jesus explains that He is the vine and we are the branches—flashes right through my mind. "This lack of identity led them to feel humiliated and embarrassed before Me," I hear Dad explain. "It was this shame they felt that led them to cover themselves up and hide from Me."

It is interesting that Adam tells God that he was afraid *because* he was naked. (See Genesis 3:10.) He doesn't just say that he is only afraid. Instead, he says that his fear is caused by the realization of his nakedness. Shame is a form of fear, and the problem is that it doesn't just lead us to believe that we are naked, flawed, disgusting, incomplete, and not good enough, but it actually takes us to a place where we try to hide our nakedness. We do not want anyone else to find out about it, not even God. Even though we try, we know that hiding it will not make it go away. So we begin to try to cover it up with something else that will hopefully give others and us the impression that we have it all together and have, therefore, been successful in curing what we all feel at some stage of our lives. Shame is only felt when we operate from our false identity, because within our true Self there is no room nor any way that shame can attach itself to us as we are complete.

When we cease to live from the tree of life, we exit the reality of our hearts. We also leave behind our true identity as we take up the task of building a false identity that will replace it. What we use to build this false identity is what I believe and like to call the modern fig leaf. There are two people in our lives today. One is our true Self who is made in the image and the likeness of God, which we can call our "I." Then, there is the false self that we work hard to build when we live our lives only from our mind and body, which we will call the "me."

To help us understand how this is played out today, we only need to take a look at Genesis 3:16 where Dad told the woman, "You'll want to please your husband, but he'll lord it over you." This word translated *please* means that there will be a "turning" in her life. When we turn, we do it toward what is most like us in proximity.

This means Dad was saying the following: "Eve, all the underlying premises you need to live a healthy and whole life, which you were receiving from Me, you are now going to turn and look to your husband to deliver them to you. This is because you came from Adam, and so this is what is closest in proximity to you." And to Adam He said, "Adam, all the underlying premises you need to live a healthy and whole life, which you were receiving from Me, you are now going to turn and look to the ground to deliver them to you. This again is because you came from the ground, and so this is what is closest in proximity to you." And so Eve turns to Adam and demands these things from him, and Adam replies, "I am not God." Adam equally turns to the ground and demands these things from it, and the ground replies, "I am not God."

To help us see this event at play in the world today, we only have to see the place women continue to look to in order to find their identity, and that is from the man they are with and how much they are liked and loved by him. Equally, men today continue to look to their careers and the success they achieve through them in order to get a clue as to their true identities.

The main opponent we face each day is not the devil, but the "me" we see each time we look in the mirror. This is the part of us we look to in order to try to understand who we are when we are not connected and living from the reality within our heart. The battle we are mainly involved in is our two opposing identities, the real "I" and the false "me," which are in conflict with each other. This is exactly what Paul wrote about in Romans 7:20: "But if I am doing the very thing I do not want, I am no longer the one doing it, but sin which dwells in me" (NASB).

The reality is that each of us is shadowed by a part of our false "me" at any given time, depending on where we are in our journey. This false "me" is what leads us to continue to invest all of our effort into the conflict within us, and much like photo-editing software, it further covers what is real and true about us.

My cigar is coming to an end, and my fingers are tired of all the typing on my iPad. As I stand up to go to bed, I know that I am about to discover what each and every one of us—who are still spiritually disconnected—is toiling so hard for. My head hits the pillow and just as my eyelids are beginning to close, I thank Dad for the awesome day and the great cigar. "Dad, tomorrow, please show me what we use to build the 'me' with," I whisper as I finally fall asleep.

My life has been mainly spent in the high end of society through my tennis career, as a player first and then as a coach on the professional women's circuit. This job has taken me to government houses, embassies, exclusive members' clubs, and it has led me to rub shoulders with movie stars, rock stars, famous personalities, and wealthy and successful people. Access into these exclusive places has given me the privilege to see better than most what the main drive behind the "me" image really looks like.

I am still a bit jet-lagged when I awaken the next day, but I am lying under the covers, staring at the ceiling now lit up by the lamp on the bedside table. "Labels," I hear Dad whisper into my heart.

"Labels?" I ask puzzled. "You mean like clothing labels?"

"Go deeper than that," He replies.

"Deeper? What do You mean?" I ask.

"Tell Me about yourself, Pablo. Who are you?"

I feel that Dad asking is a bit ridiculous. After all, He knows exactly who I am. Still, I reply by saying, "Well, I am Your son, a Christian believer, a tennis coach, a public speaker, an author." I pause for a moment before I continue: "A husband, a father, a brother, and a son. Gosh, I could go on forever, Dad."

"Yes, you could," He replies. "But that's not who you really are. Those are the labels you have been looking at to give you a clue to help you see who you have become. I didn't make those. I made your true identity within you. These labels you have mentioned are a product of what you have done through the opportunities and talents I gave you, but they are not who you really are. They are what you do, what you have become, and the roles you play every day."

I hear nothing else that morning until I arrive at the place where I am going to be sharing. As I am standing at the front, the leader of the group asks those in attendance, "Who here is Latin American, like Pablo?"

Suddenly, a voice from the back of the room says, "That's me." As soon as those two little words hit my ears, my eyes are opened to what I was shown earlier. There was my answer. The lady didn't reply by saying that is *I*. No, she said that is *me*.

I realize all those labels I had given Dad earlier were what make up the modern fig leaf I wear—what I call "me." Right then and there, before speaking, I begin to see how we look to these labels to give us the clues on how to behave and conduct ourselves, as well as how we select or treat others according to the labels they wear.

Take, for example, the label I mentioned earlier of *Christian believer*. This tells me that there is a certain code of conduct I must adhere to because this is what will be expected of me from others when they hear that I wear this particular label. Some of those behaviors will range from letting others go before me, not swearing, liking everyone I meet (including jerks), driving the speed limit, and always smiling when I arrive at church on a Sunday morning even though my wife and I have been tearing each other to shreds until we pulled into the parking lot.

Labels are the actions others will come to expect from me and I will expect from others according to the ones they wear. If either of us breaks these codes of behavior, we then use other labels to describe the person—labels like dishonest, backslider, or deceiver.

The problem with seeing things from this place is that it leads us to categorize people, which then leaves no room for the individuality that God has given to each of us and encourages us to enjoy. These labels, unfortunately, spill over into our beliefs too. And when these vary from another, we separate from them and start a new denomination that we label with a new name.

Sadly, we even fight one another in the name of our denomination and for being the one who is right and owns the truth, when in reality neither of these is possible. The saddest part about all these games is that while we are occupied serving an illusion, our true essence continues to be suppressed along with our disregard for our heart where our true Self can be found.

We go on to shape and limit our lives and the lives of others according to what we become, and not by who we really are. We further limit what we can experience by placing labels on ourselves. This is what happened to those people who labeled Jesus when, instead of seeing through the labels, they were limited by them, and the true identity of Jesus was concealed because all they could see was what His father's occupation was, whom His mother was, and whom His brothers were. (See Matthew 13:55.)

In this reality, they both worked, not to find their purpose but simply to manage and maintain the place they lived in and were a part of.

This is nothing new, and it has been happening from the day Adam and Eve ate from the tree of the knowledge of good and evil. Unfortunately, in church we often celebrate and sponsor this gathering-of-labels approach too. This is seen in how we treat those who outwardly seem more successful than others. Those who are seemingly important are given much more attention than the ones who are like the poor lady who could only give a few miserable coins. Didn't Jesus love and give priority to the poor, the sick, and the broken—the ones who didn't wear such attractive labels?

In modern times, much to-do has been made about discovering the purpose of why we are alive. Many books and manuals have been produced to supposedly help us discover what the specific thing is we are supposed to be doing. This quest has led and continues to lead many into a place where they experience frustration and a complete lack of fulfillment because they believe there is one specific thing they must do, and nothing else.

I struggled with this to the point that, at one stage, it became the very focus of my entire life. I wanted to maximize my potential and fulfill the reason I was alive. This thought gave me the idea that this would make Dad proud of me and bring Him pleasure. This unhealthy thought pattern continued until one day Dad showed me that in the Garden there was no need to find out what our purpose was, because this had nothing to do with our doing.

Adam and Eve's identity and reason for being was found in the reality they lived in, where they were aware they were one with Dad. They found everything they needed there, including their life's purpose. Adam was asked to tend and keep the Garden, and Eve was asked to be his helper. Food and water were readily available. And in this reality, they both worked, not to find their purpose but simply to manage and maintain the place they lived in and were a part of. The first time we see Adam needing to find a new identity and purpose is when, through his choices, he is driven out of the reality of the Garden that was within his heart.

This departure has led to us living in a world that prizes the outward man and his accomplishments. It is common for us to ask when we meet someone for the first time, "What do you do?" This question is directed at what people do to make money and build their false identity. But I will never forget when someone once asked me that question and I began to describe what I did for a living. After finishing, they said to me, "I didn't want to know what you did for a living; I wanted to know what you do for the world." Since then I have seen this question and my life in a different light.

Our dualistic mind takes us to a place where we separate between success and failure, between rich and poor, between extraordinary and ordinary. When we do this, we begin to compete and compare ourselves to one another, and we usually do this by measuring the worth of the labels each of us has managed to pick up along the way. We simply fail to see what Jesus meant in Luke 10:20 when He said, "Nevertheless do not rejoice in this, that the spirits are subject to you, *but rejoice that your names are recorded in heaven*" (NASB). In other words, there is no need to compete with anyone because what is truly important about this life has already been taken care of in Christ Jesus.

Furthermore, we are also led to class others according to their labels, and, in the process, we miss the reality that there are no extraordinary people in this life; only ordinary people who happen to be extraordinary at something they do. But being extraordinary at something does not mean they are better, more loved, or more favored by Dad. This might be the case before people; however, this is why I believe Jesus told us not to look for the praise of man, because He knew that this would be based on the labels we wore and not on who we really were.

Labels can change in an instant—and our worth, if it has been found in them. How can it be that someone can suddenly, because they lose a position at work, begin to feel his or her self-esteem and worth begin to waver, when within them they are still the same person made in Dad's image and in His nature? This is because the label they have just lost has left them exposed and feeling naked in the same way Adam and Eve felt in the Garden.

We measure our and others' worth, and even our and their holiness, according to what we have accomplished and not in who we really are. Such is the obsession with these labels that many of us even see God as nothing more than a "how to" tool who can be used to provide us with what we believe we need to end our quest for happiness and peace if we obtain the right labels. It is no wonder that Solomon rightly described in the book of Ecclesiastes that all of our attempts, which originate from our false identity, are nothing more than pure vanity.

We must wake up and understand that living like this leads us to become attached to life instead of engaged with it. This false identity takes us to a place where we create ideals in our mind, and then we attach ourselves to them. These can range from the ideal ice cream we like to the ideal job, material possessions, or financial situation that we believe we need to attain. There is not one thing that will be responsible for ending our quest for happiness and peace—that place where we will feel complete and whole again. Jesus Himself warned against this kind of attachment when He encouraged us to hold on loosely to all life had to offer: "If anyone wants to sue you and take your shirt, let him have your coat also" (Matthew 5:40 NASB).

Unfortunately, life doesn't always quite work out in the way we want it to. And when it doesn't, we suffer unnecessarily because we have believed the lie that unless our lives are the way they need to be, they will remain somehow incomplete and below par. Living from this false identity causes us to develop such a high degree of obsession with the fulfillment of our quest to gain the whole world that we are prepared to hurt anything and anyone in our path.

This is what Jesus warned us about when He told us to cut our hand off and take our eye out, which so many have done in error in our quest to get it right. (See Matthew 5:29.) You see, what I believe Jesus was telling us was not to literally cut our limbs off, but instead to warn us that in whatever way we are seeking happiness and pleasure that brings harm to others will ultimately lead to pain and suffering. It is better to renounce our own desire for happiness than to suffer the anguish of hurting others, which only hurts us in the end too.

If our false identity was meant to be the true one and was meant to be enough, then why do people who have so much continue to worry and be filled with anxiety? The underlying fear that accompanies all we accomplish is evidence enough that it was never meant to bring security into our lives, because it is something that can be lost. Our true identity, on the other hand, is ours forever because this part of us cannot be compromised in any way as it is fused together with God. This is why the Bible tells us that perfect love casts all fear out! (See First John 4:18.)

We are one with a God who looks at our heart and not at our labels. This is clearly seen when Dad tells Samuel when looking for the next king, "Looks aren't everything. Don't be impressed with his looks and stature. I've already eliminated him. God judges persons differently than humans do. Men and women look at the face; *God looks into the heart*" (1 Samuel 16:7).

The reality is that looking at the outward appearance has been going on from the moment Adam and Eve ate from the tree of the knowledge of good and evil. Jesus knew this reality well when we see Him changing Simon's name to Peter. Jesus says to him, *"And now I'm going to tell you who you really are:* You are Peter, a rock. This is the rock on which I will put together My church, a church so expansive with energy that not even the gates of hell will be able to keep it out."[1]

Even though Peter was now following Jesus full time, Jesus knew that Peter still saw himself as the simple fisherman he had always been. His worth and identity were still based on this "me" he had grown into. Yet Jesus was now revealing to him who he really was—what his true nature was. And Jesus does this by changing Simon's name to Peter.

In the Hebrew culture, a person's name is important because parents usually name children according to what they believe their child's life is going to be about, not because they like the way the name sounds. It is common when you meet someone in Israel for that person to ask you what your name means after you tell them your name. A name change was like saying to someone, "You know that person you and everyone else thought you were? Well, that person is not who you truly are. This new name I am giving you describes who you truly are and how you were meant to express that reality within you."

The most significant and profound virtue we have is not our knowledge, nor our modern advancements or achievements, nor our advanced modern eloquence, but it is the capacity we possess as individuals to comprehend and reflect the nature, image, and likeness of God!

Dad always calls us by our "I." Dad calls Gideon a mighty warrior while he is busy hiding under the label of a coward. David is anointed king while he labors under the label of shepherd. Then there is Saul being renamed Paul on the road to Damascus. And before Jesus is born, the angel tells Mary what the child's name should be. These are massive clues that point toward the real "I" that is within each and every one of us.

Paul spoke about this part of us in Colossians 3:10-11:

*And have put on the **new self** who is being renewed to a true knowledge according to the image of the One who created him—a renewal in which there is no distinction between Greek and Jew, circumcised and uncircumcised, barbarian, Scythian, slave and freeman, but Christ is all, and in all* (NASB).

In my own life, I have seen so much shed from the Pablo I thought I was. My life in tennis was a huge billboard I became massively attached to. For years I saw myself as a failure because I never quite made it as a player or even as what I thought was a great coach. I carried a sense of self-pity and low self-esteem because I had not quite made it to the ideal place my attached label told me I needed to be. This label was one of the biggest denominators in my journey until Dad began to open my eyes and show me this truth.

He showed me that my success in this sport was not reflective of who I was or whether I was complete or incomplete. Win or lose, my true identity was safe because it didn't depend on any label I had or could get, because that part of me can't be touched, changed, or taken away by anything from the outside. It is amazing how, little by little, I have been able to see that I am so much more than a successful tennis coach—I am complete in Him.

The most significant and profound virtue we have is not our knowledge, nor our modern advancements or achievements, nor our advanced modern eloquence, but it is the capacity we possess as individuals to comprehend and reflect the nature, image, and likeness of God! Our greatest feature is not our attractive face, our sexy body, or our fame or fancy cars or homes; it is not any label we wear or acquire; it is His glory and image residing within us.

When we live from our heart, our true Self, this truth becomes an awareness that makes our life irresistibly attractive to others. We are no longer driven by our compulsions and impulses of a lacking self-image, but instead we are able to afford ourselves the luxury of understanding we are the God-kind by design. We also begin to understand that leaving behind the illusion in which most of the world lives is difficult, and at times it can feel quite lonely. This is why Jesus told us to count the cost before we followed Him. He further drove this point home when He said,

If anyone wishes to come after Me, he must deny himself [labels], *and take up his cross and follow Me. For whoever wishes to save his life* [labels] *will lose it* ["I"]*; but whoever loses his life* [labels] *for My sake will find it* ["I"]. *For what will it profit a man if he gains the whole world* [conquers the illusion of his mind] *and forfeits his soul? Or what will a man give* [worthless labels] *in exchange for his soul* ["I"]*?* (Matthew 16:24-26 NASB)

Like Adam and Eve before us, we come into the world naked and depart from it naked as well. As I become more aware of the reality of how things truly are, I feel more comfortable with the feeling of nakedness that is coming into my life each day as I let go of the labels that have given me the illusion of identity I lived under for so many years.

Jesus spoke of the need for this false nature of ours to be shed: "Truly, truly, I say to you, unless a grain of wheat falls into the earth and dies, it remains alone; but if it dies, it bears much fruit" (John 12:24 NASB). We have a clear choice where to invest our lives and efforts. We can invest in our false self with all of its labels and attachments, or we can invest in the true Self as we let the false self shed off. As I shed the false self, I feel my true Self surface as I come into the reality of the integral life I was always meant to live—a life that starts from my heart and flows through my entire being.

I have always said that uncovering and letting go of the false "me" is not an easy path. It will be painful and often slow. However, I am confident that if we take the first step toward being liberated from this illusion we have helped build, then we will find that Dad will be a willing partner with us as we both walk into the freedom and reality of the "I" who has been within us all along.

PRAYER

God, as I look back I see how screwed up my whole approach to life has been. I can see why I felt so incomplete and even naked at times, no matter how well I did. I realize now that all my cravings and attempts for public and private significance are nothing more than evidence that I still see myself separated from You and the true identity You gave me. In fact, I can't believe I have worked so hard and gone to such lengths to improve the labels I wear.

Please help me discover my true Self within my heart. Help me, because I know that shedding this false self will be hard and even scary at times. I know it is necessary if I am going to be able to see myself as You see me. It is funny, but suddenly I can understand why every time I have told someone that I love them, I have said, "I love you" instead of "Me love you." I love You, God. I love You from that deep place where You and I continue to be one. Thank You that all along, while I couldn't, You have continued to love and see the true me through all the masks and labels I have worn. Amen.

POINT OF ACTION

Take some time to contemplate what some of the biggest labels in your life are that you have become attached to. Write down what detaching from these labels would look like in your life and how that might be practically expressed.

NOTE

1.   This is a paraphrase of Matthew 16:18.

CHAPTER 4

SEEING THE TRUTH

No man can say his eyes have had enough
of seeing, his ears their fill of hearing.
—KING SOLOMON

The moment you think you understand a
great work of art, it's dead for you.
—OSCAR WILDE

Much of what I have discovered thus far has opened my eyes to a reality that is difficult to believe I was not able to see before. How could it be that I lived for so many years as someone I thought was a devout and committed Christian, yet all along I was living under the same illusion that, although expressing it differently, most of the world is functioning under?

I read the Bible. I prayed. I tithed. I gave to the poor. I worked religiously on my behavior. And to top it all off, I even went to a Bible training school. Yet with all of these labels attached to me, I continued to miss what was really true about my life and the God I claimed to know. Many of the limitations on my life were self-imposed out of fear of the unknown. In reality, it was not that I was scared of what I didn't know, as much as I was petrified of leaving behind what I did know and had become familiar to me.

My boundaries were close and rarely did they entertain anything that didn't bear the name of Jesus, Christianity, or the endorsement that some famous preacher had given. My stance was clear. If it didn't have the right labels, looked the way I thought it should, or someone else had gone there before me, I passed it over.

This reality began to forge itself together one day while I found myself working with a player on a tennis court back home. This day, like any other day, my heart was hungry to discover more about my true Self and the One who is fused together with me. I was beginning to realize that all my hard work in keeping the illusion going, and which I thought would get me back to the reality of the Garden, was actually blinding me from the truth that was within me.

The coaching session begins as any other session does, with a conversation about the task at hand. I explain to my player that the approach she is taking is what many believe is the correct way tennis is played, but today I would like to show her a new way. I begin to open the parameters a bit, and, as I am doing this, she listens intently. I can see from her reactions that she has never heard this before. "Pablo, I have never seen tennis played like this before," she says. "What you are sharing with me today is completely alien to me. I mean, I never saw it like this or even thought that this way of playing existed."

I thanked her for her honesty and vulnerability, because most players would never be able to put their ego aside and claim to have never seen something. The session continues, and as I head home at the end of the day I hear Dad leading me to check out the story of the prodigal son.

The story of the prodigal son is a story many of us are familiar with. We all know how a young and wild son took his inheritance early and left to spend it in the fast lane of life. We also know that in the Hebrew culture, when a son does this it is the same as him saying he wished his father were dead. We are also aware of the crowd to which Jesus is telling the story—common Jews of the day who were aware of a distant God who is only happy when they do everything right and who punishes them severely when they do it wrong. At least, that was what they were probably being told every Saturday at the synagogue. We are also aware of the older son and how he resents his brother, and especially his father, when the boy returns.

The way Jesus chose to tell this story shows that He was trying to work up the crowd against the young son. He wanted their religious expectations accompanying their take on God to surface. He wanted all the anger and frustration caused by this way of approaching Dad to boil over. And He did this masterfully as He began to go into great detail about what this young man wasted away. Jesus has the crowd hanging on His every word. By the time He gets to the end of the story, their veins are pulsating on the side of their necks and their fists have turned white from clenching in anger. They can feel that right about now, the young boy is going to be slammed like they have been all along, every time they got it wrong.

Jesus finally pauses and looks at them. A moment of silence fills the place as He scans the room. They are all on the edges of their seats, focused on what is about to come out of Jesus's mouth. Suddenly, He gets up and begins to smile. No one really understands what is happening. Yet they keep focused on Him, and He suddenly raises His voice and tells them that the father runs to greet the boy. In fact, He goes on and tells them with great excitement that the father puts a new robe on him and kills the best animal in the house to throw a feast because his son has returned.

People are clearing their ears and looking at one another to make sure they have heard correctly. "Did He just say that the father did what I thought He said he did?" Yes, He did. Jesus did it because that was the whole reason behind Jesus telling this story in the way He did. It was to show them that Jesus was here to share with them a totally different and new understanding and reality about them and God.

For so long I missed the fact that the main point of the story about the prodigal son is not about what happened with the son, but about what should have happened but didn't. This is why Jesus included the elder son, whom everyone in the crowd would have related to and thus would have expected God to act in a similar manner. I can only imagine the people's reactions once they began to calm down. It is safe to say they would have been utterly puzzled and astounded in the same way that I was when I heard of this new way to approach the journey of my life.

As I finish reading the story of the prodigal son, I begin to think of the words Jesus often used when He finished sharing something with others, which was to remind them to "let him who has ears to hear, hear, and let him who has eyes to see, see." For years, I read over these words and never thought much about them apart from the obvious message they carried.

Today, however, I see something new as I am reminded, for some strange reason, of where Jesus says:

> *The eye is the lamp of the body; so then if your eye is clear, your whole body will be full of light. But if your eye is bad, your whole body will be full of darkness. If then the light that is in you is darkness, how great is the darkness!* (Matthew 6:22-23 NASB)

As I read these words again, which I have read hundreds of times before, I also notice something new. This false identity, the "me" which is sown and raised in darkness, keeps us in the dark as long as we continue to use it as the main source to help us interpret the reality of life and ourselves. The "I" within us, on the other hand, was created and fused together with the One who gave us life. This is the One who is perfect and whole and is light, and in whom no darkness is found, and whose true nature is love.

Looking at this verse again was the discovery of my true identity, the "I." Up until this point, I always believed that what Jesus was saying was that if we look at something that is dark, then the darkness contained within that thing will reflect back at us, and we will then be dark. On the other hand, if we look at something that is light, then the light contained within that thing will reflect back into us, and we will therefore have light. The problem with this approach is, who determines what is light and what is dark? If we are honest with ourselves, we can find darkness or light in whatever we choose to look at, because we all see things differently. What one considers dark might be considered light by someone else, and vice versa.

Jesus was not saying this at all. He was actually saying that if we look at something from our outer eyes, which are made up by our false identity and are wrapped up in darkness, we will see from a place in our life that is dark. And because it is dark, we will look for and find darkness in whatever we look at, and that darkness will then be reflected back into us. Equally, if we choose to see something with the eyes of our heart, from that place where we are one with Dad and which contains light, then whatever we choose to look at, we will find light in it, and that light will then be reflected back into us.

When we see with the eyes of our false identity, the "me," we see things as we think they are. Whereas, when we look at things from our true identity, the "I," we see things as they truly are because our eyes suddenly become projectors of what is within our hearts.

Let say that I am walking down the street and see a 25-year-old girl coming toward me. She is dressed provocatively, wearing lots of makeup, and her hair is waving in the wind as if she were in a movie. She is a definite looker. What I choose to see coming toward me will depend on which eyes I use to see. If I choose to look at this beautiful young woman with the eyes of my false identity, the "me," it is clear that I will find plenty of darkness in her, which will then cause darkness to be reflected back into me. However, if I choose to see her with the eyes of light from within my true identity, the "I," I will see in this young woman a 7-year-old girl who lost her dad and who never had a male figure in her life to validate her and tell her how wonderful she is. I will see in her a woman who is desperate to find the validation and love her dad couldn't provide. She, therefore, only knows that validation from others will be more likely to happen if she dresses and exposes herself in the way I just described.

Or take for example when someone becomes extremely successful at what they do. If I choose to look at them with the eyes of the "me," then I am likely to become envious of that person's success. If I choose instead to see it through the eyes of the "I," then I am more likely to be happy for him and encouraged that the God within my heart is good and loves to bless His children.

Here are two scenarios with two very different ways of seeing. Yet each way originates with us and not from something or someone else outside of us. Which way are you prone to see in such situations? Your honest answer will go a long way in showing you which identity you are currently choosing to operate from. We need to understand that when we see things with the eyes of light, then we begin to see how things truly are. We see a different reality when we see things from the same perspective as Dad.

When we wake up and see things as they truly are, we begin to see everyone around us differently. We suddenly see that everyone—no matter who they are, what they have, or what they have or have not done—carries the same image and nature of the One who is within us. The separation we all once thought existed between us begins to fade away, as we realize that what Jesus said about doing unto others as you would have them do unto you was really for our own benefit, and not so much for the benefit of our fellow man.

The truth is that we are responsible for most, if not all, of the suffering we experience in our lives. This is because when we see with the eyes of the "me," we see the world as the place where we are going to find what we think we so desperately need. We tell ourselves that our happiness and peace is inextricably linked to what we achieve and what we manage to get (labels). When we are unable to acquire these—or, worse yet, when we do manage to get them and we realize that our happiness and peace are nowhere closer to becoming a reality—we are led to try even harder. In many cases, this leads us to inflict suffering and pain on others which, in reality, is causing pain to ourselves, because we are all connected to the same vine.

Paul spoke about a small part of a body being cut off and the pain and suffering it caused the whole body as a result. He told us that the head of this body would be Christ, and the body was made up of His children. Until recently, I believed that the kids he was referring to were the ones who had put up their hand and prayed a prayer, those who have become Christians. Today, however, I realize and see that the body is made up of each and every one of us alive in this world today, whether we have become "Christians" or not. The truth is that every single individual has been made in the image and likeness of God. The only difference between those of us who understand and see that we belong and those who are unable to see is only that God has awakened us to the reality, while others are not able to see yet.

This again is why Jesus said to love everyone as we love ourselves and to do unto them as we would want them to do unto us. He understood that if we loved them, we would love Him and ourselves at the same time. From God's perspective, there is no separation or dualism here. We are in Him and He is in us. Imagine how different the whole world would look if we all loved one another the way Jesus commanded us. Wars would stop. Poverty would disappear. Many diseases would be overcome. Plain and simple, the world would be just like it was in the Garden all those years ago, before Adam and Eve were driven out of it as a consequence of the choice they made to see things in separation.

Unfortunately, this is not the case. The enemy has gone to great lengths to blind us and keep us operating from our false self. He has sold us the illusion, and often through those we think would know better, that we are somehow flawed and dirty and repulsive to God. The enemy has successfully led us to be ashamed of our humanity, so we would make the destruction of it in the name of purity and holiness our main focus. This humanity of ours is not flawed or disgusting or repulsive to God. If it were this way, then how could Christ be a human like us? The truth is that there is nothing wrong with our humanity; Dad very bluntly said it was very good when He finished making it. (See Genesis 1:31.)

The problem begins when the role we employ our humanity for is a completely different role than it was actually created for. And this erroneous approach leads us to generate from it what we all know as sin. I would like to introduce you to two different ways we can see sin. The first way of seeing sin comes from the "me" and is, therefore, false. The second way of seeing it comes from the real us, which by now we all know as the "I."

SIN THROUGH THE EYES OF "ME"	SIN THROUGH THE EYES OF THE "I"
LIE 1: Sin makes me unpresentable in the sight of God.	**TRUTH 1:** Sin is the by-product that causes all of us to fall short of understanding the freedom, love, acceptance, wholeness, peace, and well-being God has in mind for every one of us to experience.
LIE 2: Sin is a disobedient and immoral attitude.	**TRUTH 2:** Sin is the by-product of living from our false identity. It dilutes the perception of our identity as Dad's good and beautiful children.
LIE 3: God will not bless or love me, and He will continue punishing me until I get rid of all the sin in my life. (Good luck with this one.)	**TRUTH 3:** Dad's love and acceptance of each one of us does not depend on a particular point of our journey toward discovering who we truly are.
LIE 4: At the center of my being and who I really am, is a sinner.	**TRUTH 4:** Each person is overshadowed, to a certain extent, by his false self that he has built up, and when we operate from that false self, we experience a lack of balance in our lives.

SIN THROUGH THE EYES OF "ME"	SIN THROUGH THE EYES OF THE "I"
LIE 5: If it is up to me, I will always choose the way that will lead me to sin.	**TRUTH 5:** Dad's understanding of transformation has nothing to do with our behavior modification, but instead with a fundamental and profound shift in knowing and understanding who we truly are.
LIE 6: The enemy is the one responsible for making me sin.	**TRUTH 6:** The spiritual battle we all fight every day is between our false and true identities, not necessarily with the devil.
LIE 7: Sin is what separates me from God.	**TRUTH 7:** Sin is the main driver behind the illusion of separation from God, and it is what blinds us from seeing that we are not separated from Him.[1]
LIE 8: When I sin God does not hear my prayers.	**TRUTH 8:** God hears everything we say and is aware of everything we think, despite our false self, who is incapable of hearing, seeing, or knowing God would want us to believe something different.

It is interesting that when Jesus spoke to us about our freedom, He didn't point to Himself but rather to the truth. This is clearly seen in John 8:32, where Jesus says, "Then you will experience for yourselves the truth, and the truth will free you." Furthermore, Jesus once again says He will set us free, but He will do it by connecting us to the truth that is already within us.[2]

This world lives under an illusion that is powered by the mentality of getting it all right so that God loves and accepts us. One thing that is peculiar is that many within the church who try to get it right, do so from what they believe are good motives. I don't know about you, but I have always wondered where this self-driven attempt to do good came from. It is the same attempt that led the Pharisees, and even some leaders nowadays, to behavior that goes completely against what they tell others to practice.

"Dad, how does this work?" I ask.

"It came from the tree of the knowledge of good and evil," I hear.

Once I hear this, I understand that these self-imposed attempts for goodness is us trying to live up to the standard of the good part of the tree. When we approach life this way, we create a mentality that is based on what we do and what we believe. As we work hard to get it right, we build ourselves our own salvation plan that has no faith and no mystery in it, but only our obsessive and compulsive need to control everything and everyone, including God.

Once we have been captured by this illusion, better known as the quest for self-righteousness, we work hard to capture others, and we then seek to impose our truth on everyone else, telling them this is the way and there is no other. The Pharisees did it this way. And sadly, much of what goes on within the institutionalized walls these days is based on this elitist way too.

Jesus reacted strongly against this because He understood this approach led people to the illusion that they would be God to themselves and others, thus giving them the illusion they had the God-given right to judge others because they thought they were above everyone else. The motive behind this flawed approach was the main drive behind the deception the enemy sold Eve in the Garden, "You won't die. God knows that the moment you eat from that tree, you'll see what's really going on. *You'll be just like God, knowing everything, ranging all the way from good to evil.*"

The only thing that is capable of opening our eyes, so we can see how things truly are, is the truth—and not the good of the tree of the knowledge of good and evil. This is why back in the Garden of Eden there was the tree of life—the tree of truth. As long as Adam and Eve ate from it, they remained eternal and awake within the one reality of how things truly are. Their choice to see things differently meant that it was no longer attainable for them to live in this one reality, and they had to therefore leave behind the reality of the Garden. The interesting thing is that when they leave the reality of the Garden, Dad places a sword that revolves around it continuously to prevent them from entering back in, thus eating from the tree of life.

My immediate question to Dad was, "Why would Jesus point to the truth if the place where the truth can be found has a sword revolving around it?" The answer to this question came over several weeks and through several sessions of meditation and conversations with others. The conclusion I arrived at is that the sword was placed there to prevent Adam from being eternally locked into his rebellion. For us, it is there to prevent us from being able to reach the truth through our dualistic minds. In other words, as long as we seek to employ our mind and body to try to discover the truth of who Dad and we truly are, we will get close, but we will never arrive.

We can only accumulate knowledge in our mind. All that this knowledge does is add weight into our lives without making an iota of difference to our condition. In other words, we are unable to save ourselves, and this is why the cross was necessary, as it is the blood of Christ that I believe is responsible for deactivating this revolving sword, so that the way is once again open to the truth. It is the understanding that truth releases into our lives from within our heart that gives us the ability to understand ourselves, Dad, and even the lives we live. This is what is also known as salvation.

This is what Jesus was saying to Nicodemus and the Pharisees as a whole: "You guys study the Scriptures and know them inside out, yet I am standing next to you, and you can't even see Me." They were looking for Him with their minds and not their hearts. They were feeding themselves from the illusion that came through the tree of the knowledge of good and evil, not from the truth that came through the tree of life.[3]

When we eat from the tree of knowledge of good and evil, we are not able to understand. Therefore, we judge others and ourselves because we only judge what we don't understand. This way blinds us to the ability to be able to see from the "I"—from where we can see things as they truly are, not as we think they are.

Have you noticed how common it is for many of us to immediately judge others just because they sin differently than we do, instead of taking the time to look deeper than what meets our natural eyes, which would give us a clue as to why people respond the way they do? Always remember that everyone you meet is wounded and suffering in one way or another. If we see them from our false identity, we will only see them as we are. Therefore, we judge them according to their actions because this is what is important to us when we try to live by our performance.

If we see them from our true identity, however, we will be able to simply observe them. This will give us the ability to choose to love them and not judge them, just like Jesus did in His interactions. We will understand what is really happening in their lives and that their actions are simply symptoms stemming from them living from their false and broken identities.

Unfortunately, this mission—where we try to fix ourselves and the world as a whole—has led most of us to believe that the whole aim of Jesus dying on the cross was so we could enter the Kingdom of heaven when we died—suddenly finding ourselves in eternity. The truth is that Jesus did not come so we could only enter the Kingdom of God when we died, but so that we could live abundant lives here, presently living in that Kingdom, free from sin and the illusion of living from our false self, much below what God truly intended for us.

Jesus clearly and eloquently said that the Kingdom of heaven was here and within us. None of us can, nor do we need to, enter the Kingdom of heaven, because we never left it in the first place. How can we leave something that is within us? The truth is that we simply got disconnected from its reality. The Kingdom of heaven is living life in the reality of the Garden before the illusion of separation was purchased by disobedience. Therefore, none of us needs to wait until we die to experience what it is like to live a life that, as Jesus said, is not of this world, although it resides in it.

Religion is always obsessed about telling us how it finishes, because it is all about results. Jesus, on the other hand, came to tell us how it all begins, as He is all about life right here and right now. You and I—whether we see it or not—are already living in eternity. The only reason we have time in this space is so that everything does not happen at once. This, however, does not mean we have to be bound to time or live by it by putting pressure on ourselves that we have to get it right, because we don't know the day or the hour when we will die or when He will come back.

I wonder today what would happen if you could suddenly see that there is indeed nothing wrong with your true Self, if you could see that all the efforts you have been making are actually getting in the way, instead of helping you? What if you could suddenly see that this life of yours has nothing to do with becoming something, but has more to do with you rediscovering what you already are in Christ?

Would your motives and views about things like tithing change? Or how about reading the Bible and the dozens of books you read each year? Would your behavior be any different? Would you stop watching everything you say and do? Which beliefs would you let go of and which ones would you hold on to? Would you continue to go to church every Sunday? Would you keep the same friends? Would you do all that you do every day, or would that change too? Would your habits be different? Would your disciplines change? These are all very valid questions to consider, as many of them have the potential to be powered by this illusion of separation and the need to keep working at it to keep God involved and happy with us, as we continue to try to fix the sin in our lives.

The reality is that all of us need to loosen our grip around the mental image of God that we have formed in our mind, before we can ever stand a chance to begin to understand who Dad really is. This is surely what Jesus meant when he said to us that "you can't pour new wine into old wineskins" and why David said that we are to *"taste and see that the Lord is good"* (Psalm 34:8 NASB). Our mind was never designed to know and understand God. Expecting our mind to understand God is like expecting our car to fly us from Los Angeles to Tokyo. It wasn't designed to do so. When we try to use our mind to know and understand God, we are only able to put together information about Him that is made up from what we read, have experienced, hear others tell us, and find out ourselves in our own limited knowledge.

This image will always fall short, and be limited compared to who our Dad truly is. I mean, how do we start to understand things like there is no beginning or end to Him? Or that He is outside of time and also within it? How does the mind understand that? Or what about love and truth? The reality is that our mind can't and never will be able to understand these because it was not designed with that purpose. This is the main reason why, for many of us, it is so hard to relate with Dad, to hear Him, and to walk this path that many of us know as Christianity.

When we live from our minds, just like the prodigal son and his brother, we are attached to a story about ourselves that isn't true or remotely close to the one Dad is telling. Maybe we learned this story through our religious studies and practices. Maybe this story is the consequence of heartache, rejection, or certain moments in our life when we wrongly concluded something about ourselves—I am bad, I am not enough, I am inadequate, I am ugly, I am broken, I am flawed, I am defective, I am unfixable, I am stupid, I am worthless. How much of our life are we going to allow this false story to dictate? What would it mean for you to end that story today and start writing a new story that honors your worth, value, uniqueness, beauty, splendor, and God-given identity?

Today, we have a choice to make. Do we continue to follow life under the path of this same illusion of separation that will only lead to self-righteousness and destruction? Or will we choose to wake up and walk onto the narrow path that will return us back to the reality and relationship we had in the Garden, where we will find the truth that is already within us and is responsible for setting us free?

As this day comes to a close, I now understand why Paul told us—no, shouted at us—to *"wake up* from your sleep, climb out of your coffins; Christ will show you the light!"* (Ephesians 5:14).

PRAYER

God, how did I manage to get this far? I see now why the yoke can be so heavy and hard to carry. I guess it is true after all, that Your grace and Your presence has been with me all along; otherwise, I am not sure how I could have made it this far. Thank You for this, and thank You for helping me see what I am beginning to see. I know that so much of what I think and use to judge comes from my false self. I don't like it. In fact, I never did. But unfortunately, until today I didn't know there was another way. I can't believe how hard I have been with myself and others as I have gone about my quest to find perfection in how I behave, while all along missing the reality of what was within me. God, please open the eyes of my heart and help me see and discover the truth that will set me free and help me to better understand that I am loved as I am, and not as I should be. Amen.

POINT OF ACTION

As you become aware of your true Self and begin to live from this new reality, what are some of the routines and attachments you might want to shed? Focus perhaps on one particular thing that has become very obvious while you have read this chapter. Ask God to help you understand what it might look like to loosen your grip around it.

NOTES

1. This has been adapted from a blog by Jim Palmer.

2. See John 8:36, which states, "So if the Son sets you free, you are free through and through."

3. The reason so many disillusioned "Christians" are starting to look to Eastern religions for enlightenment is because they have missed the true enlightenment that the words and life of Christ have always carried. This is the direct consequence of being taught to see and process things only through their minds and not their hearts.

PART II

CHAPTER 5

INNER BLEEDING

It is not those who are healthy who need
a doctor, but those who are sick.
—JESUS

There is no coming to consciousness without pain.
—CARL JUNG

Nice match," I say as I fix my gaze on the boy who has just defeated me. He is two years older than I am, which, in junior tennis terms, is an eternity. I see him every day at a distance in the academy I attend, and he is a member of the older group I hope to be a part of one day. Still, it is just a game, and I did have some fun out there. I pick my things up and walk off the court to meet my father who has been watching me.

"Hey, Dad," I say.

"Let's go to the car," he replies with a serious voice. This walk to the car has happened before. "Pablo, you were an embarrassment today," my dad continues. "What were you thinking? How are you ever going to be a tennis player playing like that? You have

87

no guts. You should be ashamed of yourself. The problem with you is that you have it too easy. Too much is given to you. There is no way you will be this way and be my son. You are going to be how I want you to be, or I would rather see you dead!" my father screams inside our small car.

I feel trapped with nowhere to go. Hundreds of questions are being asked, and before I can answer one of them, the next three have already been asked. I feel afraid, and my mind races, trying to find something to say that will help my father calm down.

We finally arrive at the house, and I am thrown out of the car into the garage. I pick myself up and run into my room crying. My mother asks, "What happened?" Before I have a chance to answer, my father appears from behind her with one of his leather belts in his hand and begins to beat me. The beating goes on and on and on, to the point that I struggle to breathe. My mother, who is now in tears, attempts to jump in the way, but to no avail.

Nothing is going to stop my father because, in his mind, although he beats me he is really beating himself. He is full of rage and frustration from the wounds he carries, and he is now passing them on to me. After some time, he tires and yells some things over my head that I can't remember to this day. It is sufficient to say they were not along the lines of how he loves me and is proud of me. I lie there trying to cry as my little body attempts to recover from the beating I have just received. My parents go on to have a massive fight. Eventually, I crawl under my bed and spend the rest of the afternoon hiding from my dad and life as a whole. I am nine years old.

This episode repeated itself several times in my younger years, although I continued to strive to please my dad with all of my accomplishments. Every day that went by, I was further gripped by the fear of losing. For every match, my aim was to not lose, because I knew that winning meant not getting beaten when I got home. Needless to say, my game suffered as a result. Playing this way stalled my progress and severely handicapped my talents and abilities. In the smaller categories, however, I still managed to win as I ran like a marathon runner from side to side getting every ball, just waiting for my opponent to miss.

I hated tennis. I hated everything about it, but I had to keep playing because it was what I "had" to do. I preferred soccer or even motocross to tennis. At school, I was a very popular boy amongst my peers, although I was always unable to fully join their kind of life. This was because every day after school I would be on the court hitting those little yellow balls again and again. I realize now that school was an escape for me. While I was there I could feel normal and free from having "big brother" looking over my shoulder. I longed to have a normal life once again, which I did have before tennis got in the way.

"Pablo, we have decided you are going to go and stay with your grandparents in America, because tennis there is much better for you," my father and mother announced to me one day out of the blue. I had been to America before on holiday. At that time, America meant Flipper at the Miami Sea Aquarium, Mickey Mouse, Donald Duck, and Burger King—an absolute paradise. My face lit up at the news, not realizing what I would be giving up and what I was about to experience over the next several years, roaming around the world on my own, often sleeping in the houses of people I barely knew, airport floors, and even in the back of a car several times, often too broke to eat.

The day finally came to board the plane to go to America. I told all my friends goodbye, thinking how lucky I was to be going to live in this land. My father, who was a senior flight attendant at the time, was aboard the plane with me, as he happened to be working that same flight. We arrived together in America. Once at his hotel, however, he called my grandfather to come and pick me up. While we waited in the lobby, he said to me, "Pablo, you have a huge opportunity before you. If you have to return home, you will have failed and will probably live like a failure the rest of your life." I hugged him and told him that I would not let him down, I would never be coming back, and that I would go on to become the best in the world. He hugged me back. I stared down at the ground, wondering what this really meant. I was 13 years old.

My father gave to me what had been given to him. This, unfortunately, is the way life goes unless we awaken to the reality of who we truly are in Christ. The beatings and all the added mental and emotional stress I underwent were done—believe it or not—with my good in mind, even if the impact on my life was quite the opposite. My father acted out of the love he had for me. He wanted the best for me, and this desire mixed with his shortcomings as a man meant that they were expressed in a way that did not deliver the outcome any of us hoped for.

Upon arrival at the house, I hugged my grandmother and my cousin, whom I really liked because he was like the brother I never had, being a year younger than me.[1] My first few days in America were great, until it was time to get back to tennis. My father had arranged for a friend of his to introduce me to the tennis scene and open doors of opportunity. Unfortunately, he was a charlatan and never did as promised. This meant I had to start to play at a local facility where the coaching was terrible.

After a few weeks, school started and I could barely speak English in a country where kids dressed, acted, looked, and even danced differently. I will never forget the embarrassment I felt the first day I walked into my junior high school. Girls began to make fun of my English, or the lack of it. The boys were only too happy to impose their authority over the new kid. I wanted to die. I felt so rejected and was deeply wounded by this experience. This continued every year until I got to my senior year in which I finally began to gain some popularity, although it was nothing like I had back home.

All these experiences meant that my aim was firmly fixed on finding a place to belong and be accepted so I could just be one more in the crowd. This, unfortunately, became impossible because I moved around and attended a different school every year, trying to fit my studies around my ever-changing tennis base and coaching arrangements. With every change, the whole cycle repeated itself—new school, new place, new friends or lack thereof, and a completely new life to get settled into. With each of these changes, I became more and more unstable and angry by the minute.

The wounds I had picked up when I was being abused continued as I experienced the same treatment at the hands of others who didn't know any better. What was a young boy—in a country that was not his own, with people he had never met, and with extremely limited resources—expected to do? The reality is that the aim of the whole exercise was to turn me into a world-class tennis player. Yet all it did was murder my emotions.

These wounds drove and ruled my life. Like all wounded people, I began to search for comfort zones where I could retreat from the constant pain that accompanied my life. All along, I was blind that within me life was bleeding away. No matter what I did, it was never enough to calm the raging waters. I tried so hard to get it right, yet I failed. Still, I could not go back home because there was no way I was going to be a failure in my dad's eyes.

Most nights when I went to bed, I longed for the tender touch and reassurance of my mom and dad. But all I got was the dark empty room. Every time I ran into a problem, I learned to solve it myself. And with each passing day, I learned to survive without my parents. They became distant friends I used to live with— nothing more. As far as I was concerned, I was it and I had to somehow make it all work. Going back home was not an option.

The quest to heal myself led me to some dark places. I spent many years doing drugs and drinking at a young age, all the time pretending I was a clean and upstanding athlete. I attempted to cure the embarrassment I had received from my earlier years in school, mainly at the hands of girls, by having multiple promiscuous relationships. To this I added pornography, which gave me the sense of total control, power, and comfort, until the video came to an end. I did things I am not proud of; I went places and got involved and influenced by people I now see as a grave mistake. I had become a deeply wounded young man who saw every opportunity as a chance to make it to that place where I was told it would be okay. And with every failed attempt, the dream faded further away.

As an adult, I was driven to make decisions that had nothing to do with love or desire, but more with impulses, compulsions, and addictions. I can now see how my first marriage was an attempt to create the home environment I didn't have as a child. I honestly thought I loved my first wife, but I can see now that we were both deeply wounded and needed each other more than we could have ever loved each other. At least, this was the case from my side as I looked for comfort from the inner bleeding that had been going on within me since that disastrous day when my dad first beat me.

Not only that, but I inflicted this pain and wounding onto my first three kids as well. My approach to parenthood, although not as extreme as my father's, nevertheless resembled his traits of demanding top-tier performance from my kids, especially from my first daughter and son. I alienated them and caused them to mistrust me because they knew they could not be real with me— all I was interested in was their perfect behavior and results.

Becoming a Christian did not cure me, as I transferred my wound management and attempts for self-healing to managing a relationship with a God I saw in the same way as my father. While God was interested in my heart, in healing my life, and in showing me how much He loved me, I was more interested in Him helping me get it right so I could finally fulfill my dream— well, nightmare by now—of making it in life. It didn't matter at what, just as long as it was big, loud, and noticeable.

Religion only added to this pain, because instead of dealing with my wounded heart, it dealt with me. I worked so hard to cure and fix the symptoms in my life that had developed into destructive habits. I thought the answer would be in behavior modification. How wrong I was and how much pain I inflicted while I continued to hurt others and myself in the name of finding the happiness and peace often promised—if I just got it right.

Most, if not all, of our compulsions, addictions, and impulses are the symptoms and by-products of us feeding our soul through our mind and flesh, instead of using our heart and spirit. The source that powers these behaviors and drives us to the great lengths we go to in order to satisfy ourselves are the wounds we carry with us. They are responsible for keeping us disconnected from our new heart and preventing it from feeding our soul.

It is important to understand that for centuries the majority of the saints have focused all of their efforts on fighting these symptoms in the hopes of somehow finding a permanent cure and relief. Many books have been written, sermons preached, and counseling sessions attended in the hopes of extending some much-needed tools to help fix these symptoms, which are responsible for bringing so much shame into our lives. And this will continue to happen as long as we make it about right and wrong, as all the law is able to do is point out and try to fix the symptoms, not our wounded hearts.

Ultimately, the reality for us is that whatever we give our attention to we empower over ourselves. I could share about many unhealthy habits, because I had most of them; however, I have chosen to focus on one habit I was set free from and which I know most men struggle with, including those who think they are too holy to admit it. This is the habit of pornography.

Many of us who struggle with this habit will know that it can be unrelenting. We fight it for a week and successfully stay away from it, then unexpected bad news or even a bad day at work brings us right back into it without any hesitation. Often, when this happens, we not only return to it, but we do it with a vengeance. Then a gut-wrenching guilt and the same battle to get to where we were a week ago follows. For some of us, this has been our experience for decades; for others of us, maybe only months. No matter what we try, it will just not go away. I know because I lived like this for many years.

While I traveled, I had many lonely nights in hotel rooms. I was making progress in my spiritual life, but at the same time I had found a comfort pill with porn. It was freely available on the Internet, and my Bose headphones meant that I could envelope myself into my own erotic private cyber world without anyone else knowing. I knew this was not beneficial for me, and I also knew that I had a problem, but I didn't dare discuss it with anyone, not even God. I thought I was the only one with this problem, even though the porn industry earns billions of dollars each year. I surely wasn't responsible for all of those profits.

I will never forget the day I was set free from this addiction.[2] I find myself inside a room in a very expensive hotel. It has been a long and difficult day. I take a shower and order some room service. After eating, I lie back on my bed and turn on my laptop and begin to inject myself with another dose of my comfort pill. As I start watching a short video, I close my computer and try to pray. I pray but the urge is just too much, so I open the laptop again and continue watching.

I watch more than a dozen videos and try to repent again and again, but there is no use because by now I am totally overtaken by it. I realize that the clock has reached midnight, and I need to go to bed. I eventually switch the computer off and put the headphones down on the bedside table. My head hits the pillow and tears of shame and pain are streaming down my face. I feel so lonely and distant from everything and everyone I care about and love. I am in the middle of nowhere, and the guilt running through my mind is on overdrive. It is going to be another sleepless night.

I fight so hard to get rid of these feelings and voices that torment me for doing the very thing that brought me comfort. "How can You love and like me, Dad, after another night like this," I whisper as my eyelids are finally closing.

"That's the problem, Pablo," I suddenly hear in my heart.

I quickly awake. "What is the problem?" I ask.

Dad replies, "That you don't understand how much I love you, even while you are in the middle of doing it."

I realize with this last statement that what Dad is trying to show me is the more I fight this temptation, the more I feed the illusion that He is separated from me and displeased with me while I indulge myself. I also notice for the first time that I am the one who is responsible for strengthening and empowering this habit by trying to fix it myself. I then sense the strangest thing I have ever felt in my life—Dad reminding me of something He showed me in the past.

Some time back I was reading John 13:3-10, the story where Jesus washed Peter's feet, when I suddenly was given insight to what I believe was the motive within the heart of Christ in that exact moment. Suddenly, I saw the whole passage capture a completely different meaning.

I had learned that in the Hebrew culture, the feet were the dirtiest and most unpresentable part of the body. This is because they are in direct contact with the ground. In Jesus's time, people didn't have Reeboks or Nikes to protect their feet. They traveled and walked on dirt roads and tracks. They went to the toilet in the bushes where things splashed all over. To this, add the heat in the Middle East and how it causes people to sweat. Such was the stench and state of their feet that they didn't wash their faces or hands when they entered someone's house without first washing their feet.

So here is Jesus kneeling in front of Peter. He has a bowl of water and a cloth. He looks at him and, as He lowers His eyes, He grabs his feet, and begins to wash them. Suddenly, as I am reading this, I hear Dad tell me, "This is where I want to start in your life, Pablo."

"My feet?" I ask.

"No, I want to start with the dirtiest, most unpresentable part of you," He replies. "You know that part of you that you are the most ashamed of. Here is where I want you to understand the most how much and how well I love and accept you." My world stops once I realize that Dad is showing me that He not only knows about the dark side of my life, but He is not ashamed of it.

I am fully awake and sitting up in my hotel bed now. As I rehearse the passage of Jesus washing Peter's feet, I realize I need to stop fighting this habit and I need to allow Dad to join me in the middle of it. What I proceed to do next is open my laptop and start watching videos again. I watch dozens of them until the early hours of the morning. The strange thing is that this time I don't feel guilt anymore. By video number ten, I begin to feel loved and affirmed. It is almost as if Jesus is sitting next to me, looking straight at me with His arms around me. This feeling only grows as the number of videos increases, until I suddenly push the laptop away and stop. The guilt and condemnation are gone, and so is the impulse and drive to watch. I switch the computer off and get back into bed. The room is dark, and I lie there staring at the ceiling. I feel comforted and loved. I feel no shame as I realize that light has shone into this part of my darkness for the first time in my life.

> We need to realize that when we battle our sin, our back is to the cross. But when we stop battling our sin in our own willpower, we turn our attention to the cross and give our backs to the sin that entangles us.

I can understand how—by this stage—you, the reader, must be thinking there is no way this can be the way to see freedom and healing from this habit or any other habit you might be struggling with. You are probably thinking there is no way you could ever invite God to be with you while you indulge yourself in your dark secrets. I understand this reaction because this is the same reaction Peter had when he said to Jesus, "You will never wash my feet, Lord." My advice to you is that you take the time to consider what Jesus said next to Peter, which I believe is the same thing He said to me and He is saying to you at this moment in time:

"If I don't wash you, you can't be part of what I'm doing."

Think about this for a minute. What would it take to let Jesus wash your life with his loving and healing hands?

As Jesus washed me during this groundbreaking night in the hotel room, much healing and relief was brought into my soul. Starting that night, my habit gradually decreased to the point where, some weeks later, it completely disappeared altogether. I knew I was loved, and I also knew that this was true even though

Dad knew about my habit. We need to understand that it is not the power of God that changes us, but the presence of His love within us that empowers us to overcome the habits that overpower us.

When I watched these videos and was conscious of Jesus's presence, something broke within me that then led me to be able to see what the real problem was. The moment we embrace and accept those parts of us that we fight so much to get rid of, we suddenly and swiftly render them powerless. This happens because the minute we accept them as they are and not as they should be, we walk into the embrace of the Father. This embrace exposes us to the love of God, which is what we empower over ourselves and the habit we struggle with. Thus the love of God is empowered in our lives as we experience His love for us in the midst of our darkness.

We need to realize that when we battle our sin, our back is to the cross. But when we stop battling our sin in our own willpower, we turn our attention to the cross and give our backs to the sin that entangles us. This sudden shift in attention brings us to the place where Dad can begin to show us the wounds within our lives, and we are now able to pay attention to them instead of the symptoms we fought for so long. Dad tried to show me my wounding through my behavior. Yet I was so focused on fixing the symptoms that I was unable to see the life that was bleeding out of my heart.

Seeing our wounds takes time—and it takes even longer time to understand them. I thank Dad for grace, because without it there is no way one could undertake this long process that seems like one continuous failure after another. Yet the reality is that each time we fail, we are actually getting closer to the place where we will understand and see past the symptoms, to what is really happening within. I can now see how priceless clues about the wounds in my life were contained all along within sudden and unexpected bursts of anger.

"Hi, darling," I say to my wife Madeleine, as I give her a kiss and enter the car. She has just picked me up from the place where I have been doing some coaching. During the last 15 minutes of my last lesson, I have been looking forward to going with her to pick up my daughter from school, because this is what my wife and I agreed we would do that morning.

We begin to talk about the day we have each had, and all is well within the Giacopelli four by four. Suddenly, out of nowhere, my wife tells me that her dad, who hasn't seen Gisella for a little while now, is in the area because of work, and he would like to meet her and say hi when she comes out of school, spending some time with her before coming home. And because she knew that I don't like to hang around the shopping center where the school is, she wondered if I would prefer to go home first and wait there for them. The minute I hear all of this, something within me erupts like a volcano; I completely and utterly lose myself. I begin to scream and accuse her of putting her father before me. I tell her that I am sick of her rejecting me in this way, and that she always thinks about others before me.

Her tone of voice was gentle. There was absolutely no malice or anger on her part. She was simply thinking about everyone concerned and had figured this was the best way to do it. For me, however, I saw it as a deliberate attempt to reject me, which led to my wounds of abandonment and isolation. Madeleine is now crying, and I am beside myself. I arrive outside the building where we live and exit the car, blaring out some very colorful language. As the door slams behind me, I enter the complex still fuming.

After fumbling into the apartment, I find a cigar, open a beer, and go sit outside on the balcony. After several puffs, I begin to calm down and quiet myself from the Oscar-winning performance I just put on. "Do you remember asking Me to show you why you struggled for so long with your habit and why you have so much anger?" Dad suddenly whispers into my heart.

"Yes, I do remember," I reply—not exactly happy to hear it at this moment.

"Well, you have just seen it at work," Dad says.

"What do you mean?" I ask puzzled.

"Pablo, when you were beaten as a kid for losing a match and then sent away from your home, you felt rejected," Dad continues. "This rejection, over the years, turned into abandonment as you realized you didn't have anyone or anywhere to turn to. You tried to find your home everywhere you went and everywhere you stayed, but for one reason or another, it didn't happen."

He continues, "When Madeleine spoke to you today, you responded with your wound. Your response had nothing to do with what she said, but was more about your understanding of the situation. When you are wounded, you interpret everything through your wound. The wound conditions your life and even leads you to create situations where you end up being hurt in the same way you are wounded. So if you have a wound of rejection, then you will always look to create situations that will cause others to reject you and make you feel rejected. If you continue to do this, you will eventually find your identity in being a reject."

"So where did it all this start?" I naturally ask. After asking this simple question, Dad brings to mind specific events I went through in my younger years where I was wounded, not just by one person but by several—situations where I was rejected by those I loved. Each situation Dad shows me is painful. Vivid pictures begin to crowd my mind, and I see the offenses taking place. Tears are flowing down my cheeks as I begin to realize where all this pain in my life has come from. I cry for a long while—often with groans—as painful and unhealthy emotions are set free. As my crying subsides, I pick my gaze up and stare at the ocean in front of me. I feel a soothing stroke of Dad's invisible hand. I am suddenly seeing that wounded kid, who has been frantically bouncing inside the prison of his wounds, begin to depart from my life.

"Dad, thank You so much," I say. "I am so grateful for this moment. Thank You for having the ability to heal and set us free that no psychologist, counselor, or layman has." I spend some more time sitting there, enjoying this feeling of health and cleanness for the first time in my life. As I begin to get up from my chair to come back inside so I can call my wife to apologize for my outburst, Dad gently whispers into my heart, "I am so proud of you. I love you, Pablo. I am happy that you are alive."

In the days ahead, as I enjoy my healing, I also began to realize that even though I felt free, my life and my thinking are often pulled back toward the same mentality I possessed when I was wounded. "Why is this happening, Dad?" I ask. Dad points me to the passage in Scripture in Luke 11:24-26 where Jesus talks about the house being swept clean and overtaken.

"There is something else we need to take care of, Pablo," Dad says.

"What is that?" I ask.

Following a long pause, Dad says, "I will show you."

PRAYER

God, so much is now beginning to make sense in my life. For so long I have hidden these feelings and impulses, wondering if they would ever go away. Please help me walk into the darkest part of my heart hand in hand with You. As we do this, please remind me that despite the shame I feel around others about my past, You are not ashamed of it, and I should not be either. Help me to see what You see and feel what You feel toward me, even when I am in the middle of doing what You know I am not proud of. I have so much to work through, but today I know that what matters is that we have started the process. I know I am going to have to face shame and guilt, which I have allowed within my wounds. Please help me when this happens.

Forgive me for trying to manipulate my life by having a go at fixing the symptoms of my wounds. I realize that these wounds are not all my fault, but because of them I have wounded others. I want to thank You, God, for what You are doing in my life and in my heart, and the way this new place is changing me. Amen.

POINT OF ACTION

Go for a walk outside in the countryside, beach, or mountains. Find a spot, preferably one that is wide open and uninhibited, where you will be able to spend some time on your own. When you find this spot, take it in for a while before you begin to ask God to show you how He would like to deal with the wounds in your heart. I encourage you to write down what God reveals to you as together you work through the suffering that has held you back.

NOTES

1. My grandparents raised my cousin because his own parents were unable to raise him.

2. Please understand that this is my own story of how Dad dealt with me. I have shared this story with others and, like me, they too have been able to see healing and freedom from it and the guilt that accompanies it. That said, it is important that you ask Dad for your own revelation, even if it's along the lines of what I am going to share next.

CHAPTER 6

BREAKING THE DEAL UP

...and when it comes, it finds it
swept and put in order.
—Jesus

I wear the chain I forged in life. I made
it link-by-link, and yard-by-yard.
—Charles Dickens

A lovely melody awakens me as I hear my phone ringing. It is Friday morning, which means it is the beginning of the weekend here in Israel. "Hello," I say, answering the phone.

"May I speak with Mr. Pablo Giacopelli, please?" the voice with a heavy English accent says on the other end.

"Speaking," I say.

"Sir, I am calling about an agreement you made some time ago with the bank," the man says.

"What agreement?" I ask, because I don't remember ever making one.

The man goes on to explain that this was done through a conversation with my account manager, and that because a review of all accounts was taking place, they thought they should contact me. He goes on to tell me that because of this agreement (which I didn't make), I had paid the bank a certain amount of money over the years.

"How can that be possible if I never agreed to it?" I ask.

"Well, you seem to have at some stage, sir. Would you like to cancel it?" he replies.

"Too right I want to cancel it," I say.

After talking a bit longer, I hang up the phone. I realize that for the last several years, I have been paying a nominal fee without even knowing it. Since switching to online banking, these fees are kept somewhere else on the information dashboard panel, which I don't have a clue where that is exactly. I lie in bed for a while longer, trying to enjoy the first moments of my morning after the surprise phone call. The kids are playing and my wife is with them.

"Good morning, Dad," I say.

"That's not the only agreement you have made that you are unaware of," I hear in my heart.

"What do you mean?" I ask.

"Remember I said there was something else we needed to take care of?" He replies.

"Yes, I do remember, and I remember You said You would show me," I say. As I lie there, my eyes are opened to see that what I have just witnessed through the phone call is something that has clearly extended itself into my life and has reached far beyond my bank account.

I have spent many moments crying since that day on my balcony, feeling the hands of God healing different wounds in my life. These wounds have been hiding something far more sinister than any wound I have carried within.

I now understand that wounding leads us to make agreements and vows, which in time, develop into a fundamental belief system about ourselves. This lie and illusion lurks at the very bottom of our lives from where it permeates the whole of our beings, much like a leaking bottle of water spreads its contents slowly over a cloth until it completely takes over. This belief system develops into a part of our false identity that we then relate and identify with. All our dealings are marred by it. Its shadow towers over us. Our relationships are contaminated by it, and the aromas of our lives carry this underlying stench within it. The most tragic part of all is that this belief system becomes a god we ultimately submit to and serve, as it battles for our loyalty toward this illusion we have believed and integrated much of ourselves into.

I think of all the years I was consumed with trying to fix the symptoms of my wounds, how often I punished myself until I became the judge of my life instead of an observer and student of it. Each time I set for myself the highest standards, believing this was what Dad wanted all along. The only change that happened, however, was how tired and burnt out I became. With each wound that I have worked through, a new part of my heart has resurfaced. But as I've shared before, I still find myself being taken into negative patterns of thinking, and I was about to find out why and how these got here.

"Dad, what are these agreements I have made?" I ask.

With my eyes closed, a scene comes into my mind. I am taken back to that first time I was beaten up for losing a tennis match. I see myself dragging myself under the bed. I see how I begin to tell myself that the only way I will be loved and embraced will be for me to win every time. Furthermore I tell myself that I am a loser, as self-pity begins to seep into my being. I accept the accusation that I am responsible for my dad getting upset and for my parents fighting. By the time I emerge from under the bed, I have initiated several vows. I have accepted a set of lies about myself that, over time, will be strengthened as I face these situations once again and not just at home, but with others too. I lie in bed weeping and distressed, and I realize how robbed my life has been.

Then another picture surfaces from some years later when I was living with my grandparents. I am sitting outside on my granddad's truck; the tailgate is open. My cousin approaches us, and my granddad tells him that he has booked him lessons to learn how to fly an airplane. My eyes nearly pop out of my head, and I begin to think that he will next tell me that I am also coming along with him. But that never happens. I wait while they talk about it, and then I ask with a great big innocent smile of expectation, "Granddad, can I come too? Please."

My grandfather turns to me and says, "Your father can pay for you to do that because I won't." His words travel through my heart as a dagger slashes the flesh of a soldier at war. I mean, come on, I am his grandson too. I live with him. I am also a boy who wants to have fun and discover new things. He supposedly loves us both the same, right? I feel the same feeling as in past situations as I relive this scene of abandonment and utter rejection. While my cousin laughs at me, I see myself run into the house and into my room where I begin to cement over the same feelings I felt while under my bed years before.

This morning, I feel led to speak out and renounce the vows I have made and forgive the offending parties. One by one I address them and break them off in the name of Jesus. I renounce the rejection and the lies I bought into that everyone and everything would reject me as long as I lived. The fear of abandonment is loosened from my life. I begin to weep from the sense of understanding and belonging, of not being alone.

"Pablo, this is what I was saying to you when you were in the middle of these situations," Dad speaks into my heart. He begins to show me what the truth was about me then as it is now. I hear Him whisper truth about my life, and with each spoken word I sense a new awareness of freedom. I was not only breaking the vows, but in their place truth was surfacing, and it was setting me free.

My emotions are all over the place as I face much of the hidden pain that has been responsible for causing most of the suffering I have experienced in my life. I realize that I am reaching into the very depths of my being while I navigate with Dad into the troubled waters in my heart.

Suddenly, like an empty bottle surfaces from under the water, the word *loser* pops up into my being. "What is that, Dad?" I manage to ask. But before He can answer, I begin to speak with utter conviction about what I now understand is the core belief I had adopted about my persona: "I am a loser. I am no good. I am a failure. I will never make it in anything. I have nothing to show for my life and never will," I say, anger growing with each spoken word.

"Keep going, Pablo," I hear Dad whisper. As I continue to speak, I begin to weep again, swearing and cursing over these lies that have been responsible for disabling my life for so many years. Within me, there are feelings of disappointment, frustration, joy, and exuberance. This belief was the very thing that was responsible for poisoning the view I had of myself, others, and Dad.

"You are not a loser, Pablo," I hear Dad speak into my heart. "You are My beloved son." I weep again as these words are the truth, and they hit the spot like nothing else can.

"**** you, Satan! You are the ******* loser! You muppet!" I shout from the top of my lungs. I can't believe I have just said that, but this is what comes out of my mouth. I feel sudden bursts of energy and courage I have never felt before. Something new is emerging within me, healing in the depths of my being. As this is happening, the Scripture of the house being swept clean and over-taken again comes to mind:

> When a corrupting spirit is expelled from someone, it drifts along through the desert looking for an oasis, some unsuspecting soul it can bedevil. When it doesn't find anyone, it says, "I'll go back to my old haunt." On return, it finds the person swept and dusted, but vacant. It then runs out and rounds up seven other spirits dirtier than itself and they all move in, whooping it up. That person ends up far worse than if he'd never gotten cleaned up in the first place (Luke 11:24-26).

I understand this time that the truth Dad has just spoken into my life is what has been missing. The absence of it is what has led me to continue to struggle after the wounds were revealed for the first time on my balcony. This is the truth that was responsible for setting me free and keeping me free, and it would act as an antidote in the future when the vows and lies would try to return.

With most healing processes, there is one final step that many of us are unaware of—how our emotional growth is suppressed by our wounds and the vows we have made. One day, I discovered this as I was driving out of the underground parking lot of the building in which I live.

For some time, I had realized there was something I struggled with in Israel, but I didn't know what it was. Something within this society was putting its finger on a part of me that, although I was aware of it, I could not figure out what it was. Much time has gone by without any clarity until this winter morning. I was driving around the corner onto the ramp that would take me to the road, when a scene from my childhood entered my mind.

I was at the beach back in South America. I am guessing I was around seven years old. At the beach, I find myself with my aunt, who is now deceased, and her son, the same cousin I mentioned earlier. I was sitting in the perimeter of the tents and umbrellas our family had erected. My parents, aunt, and other adults were shooting the breeze while my cousin and I played in the sand.

My aunt begins to tell a story about something she had witnessed in a parking lot earlier that week. She tells everyone that this old man in his brand-new Mercedes was waiting for another vehicle to exit the space he wanted to park in. While he waits, someone else comes from the other side of the parking lot and pulls into the now empty space the man had been waiting for.

The woman inside the car gets out, looks at him, and laughs as she shouts, "The world belongs to those of us who are quick!" The old man places his Mercedes in reverse, and, as he puts it back into drive, he accelerates and crashes into the lady's car. He does this again and again as the lady watches from the side, completely outraged.

My aunt had by now safely backed up her car and was witnessing all of this from a distance. She notices that once the old man is finished, he gets out of the car, walks up to the woman, and as he hands her a business card, he says to her, "The world does not belong to those who are quick. The world belongs to those who are rich." He then continues, "Here is my secretary's number. Call her and she will see to it that your car is fixed." Everyone in the tent and under the umbrellas, including my cousin and me, are speechless as we were hanging on her every word.

After hearing this story, I bought into another lie. This lie became a belief that had been ruling my life until this winter morning, when I understood that what has troubled me so much about this country is the amount of money and success most people have. This belief has conveniently lodged itself with the belief of being a loser. I believed the way a man's worth was measured was through how much money and success he had.

I renounce this lie and begin to speak truth over my life as I hear it within my heart. I am amazed how a simple and innocent story I overheard had such an impact in my life. As I look back on my life, I see how my financial position, though better than most, has been responsible for fueling my low self-esteem. Yes, I had money, but I was by no means rich. The man in the story had said *rich*, and I knew I was not that—at least not if the size of my wallet was the measure.

I sigh deeply as I feel once again freed from something that was dormant as far as I was concerned, but was very much active for a little more than three decades. Continuing to drive for a short while, I begin to realize that in every time I have seen a scene about my wounds and vows, I am always a child. "Why is that, Dad? Why am I not the age I am today? I realize I was a kid then, but am I no longer a kid?" I ask.

"In those areas you remain a kid until you allow Me to set you free," Dad replies.

Dad was showing me that something else happens to us when we are wounded and agree to a vow or a lie. In my case, the wound that was inflicted on me when I was nine was inflicted at the hands of someone who loved me unconditionally, and I looked up to and loved him with all of my heart. This not only wounded me, but it caused my emotional growth in that part of me to stop. As Dad showed me this, the immature way I often behaved in so many situations when I felt rejected and inferior to others began to make more sense. I now understood that it was not me who was facing it, but the nine-year-old boy within me.

This small boy, like most that age, was incapable of handling these emotions and situations like an adult. So each time they happened, the response was similar to that of a nine-year-old. He felt less than others. He somehow felt incomplete, and so he responded by acting like a child who didn't receive the same toy his brother did on Christmas morning. Every time I have experienced a similar situation, I find myself talking to the nine-year-old boy within me. And each time I do this, I feel myself grow.

This labyrinth of wounds is one of the biggest dimensions responsible for bringing so much pain into our lives and the lives of others who cross our paths. As with everything in Dad's economy, thank goodness nothing is wasted, not even the pain we receive and inflict on others through our subconscious actions and inopportune words. One of the biggest ways in which Dad uses the pain we experience in life is to reveal the pain we already have within us. C.S. Lewis said it this way, "Pain insists upon being attended to. God whispers to us in our pleasures, speaks in our conscience, but shouts in our pains: it is His megaphone to rouse a deaf world."[1]

Some years ago, a player of mine suffered a stress fracture in one of her legs. Every time anyone even ran his or her hands over the place of the fracture, she would respond in a very dramatic way due to the amount of pain. I will never forget one day when an onlooker approached me and said, "That was a little over the top," referring to her response as he bumped into her.

"Do you realize what is under that area you bumped into?" I ask him.

"Yeah, a bone and some muscles," he responds, trying to be clever.

"Correct," I say. "And that bone is nearly broken."

"Oh, I am so sorry," he says with a look of sorrow on his face. "I didn't realize that."

Every person we meet is suffering and in pain in one way or another. Few are the ones who have seen some degree of healing and freedom from the pain they and others have inflicted upon them. Fewer still will ever take the time to ask Dad to reveal to them what is holding them hostage.

The truth will not be able to set us free until we realize what lies are holding us captive. When a broken part of us is touched by something someone said or did, or perhaps didn't say or do, our reaction will be a huge sign of what is really going on in our hearts. What comes out of our mouths when pressed will also be a huge clue of what is going on within, as our mouths are usually the main exhaust pipe where we vent our pain. This is what happened in the car with my wife when I exploded in anger. I saw her innocent actions through the lens of my vows, which led me to see them as a trespass, even though they were not intended that way. They caused pain because they had touched a painful and wounded part within me. If I had been healthy, I would have seen them for what they were, and my heart would have received them as such because no pain would have been trampled upon.

The reality is that we will all experience pain. That's part of life and part of sharing the planet with more than seven billion broken people. Broken people break people—that's just how it is. We reproduce after our kind, which applies to our pain as much as to anything else in our lives. But Dad, in His goodness, uses pain to heal pain. We see this mentioned in Isaiah 66:9 where Dad says, "In the same way I will not cause pain without allowing something new to be born" (NCV).

As I thought about this verse, Dad reminded me of the way the fires in the oil fields in the first Gulf War had been extinguished. Saddam Hussein, as he fled Kuwait, commanded his forces to light up the oil fields. The American troops, after securing the fields, began to try to turn off the raging fire, as the potential ecological disaster was great. They tried water, they tried sand, and they tried many other things, all of which didn't work. One day, however, one of the fire specialists asked, "Why don't we fight fire with fire?" The idea seemed stupid, but they had tried everything else and had made little progress, so they decided to give it a go. I will never forget the news channels when they began to hail this discovery as a major breakthrough. Each and every oil field was extinguished as explosives were placed as close as possible to the flames and blown up. They used fire to extinguish fire. In much the same way, Dad uses pain to heal pain.

> Our wounds and vows, if left untouched, will run our lives. They will keep us as individuals who constantly need and demand attention and reassurance from those around us.

When we are exposed to pain, we have a choice to make: We can either fight it or we can face it by walking right into the middle of it. If we choose the latter, though it will be painful in the moment, we will gain understanding as we give Dad a chance to speak to us and show us what's broken within us and why. Much of the anger, anguish, and fear the pain in our lives creates is nothing more than evidence that we have a heart that is deeply wounded and broken. This wounding causes our heart to become a brewing place where unhealthy emotions thrive. Simply asking Dad to take these away won't work because all these unhealthy emotions are healthy ones turned inside out.

As healing began to flow through my life, the anger I struggled with began to express itself as righteous defiance. My anguish started to turn into a deep passion for the truth and life, and my oppressive fear started to turn into a ferocious love for others. Dad does not want to take away our emotions, He wants to heal them, and this usually happens when we first allow Him to heal the pain that is within us. We need to understand that pain is not meant to be a constant companion in our lives, but it is meant to be a visitor. It is designed, if approached the right way, to clear the way for something true and healthy to take its place. The only reason pain remains with us is because we choose to hold on to it tightly, and we often do this because this is where we have found and based our identity.

The reality is that our wounds and vows, if left untouched, will run our lives. They will keep us as individuals who constantly need and demand attention and reassurance from those around us. In our desperation, we will be unable to love ourselves, others, or even God, because it is impossible to love someone genuinely when we need him or her. I know some of you are thinking, "Well, I need God, and I will always need God." Yes, this is true. But when our eyes are opened, and we come into the reality that He is one with us, then our mental need of Him disappears and we come into the reality of who we are in Him and who He is in us. When we need someone, the fulfillment of the need will always be more important than the love we can give them or they can give us. When we are in pain and are suffering, we are not capable of seeing love for what it truly is.

This truth was further shown to me when I discovered what the word *love* originally meant in the Hebrew language, which has a completely different meaning than the definition developed by most of the rest of the world. Based on the numerical value of the Hebrew letters, the Torah shows us that the first time the middle letter is used to help make up the word *love*, it means for one "to give to another"—not to give in order to get, like we do when we are in need, but to give unselfishly.

For example, when we say we love fish, what we are really saying is that we love ourselves, because in reality what we mean is that we love the feeling and the taste of the fish in our mouths, and the satisfaction it brings once it is swallowed. If we truly loved the fish in the sense of giving unselfishly, then we would throw the fish back in the water and let it continue its life. In the same way, when we say we love someone, what we are really saying is we love the way it feels when he or she meets our needs. This is why Jesus said to do unto others as we would want them to do unto us.

The problem, however, is that when we are wounded, we can't do this because our heart is shut down and incapable of loving in a healthy way. We need to understand that even when we choose to do life away from our hearts, the enemy continues to work hard to destroy us through the wounding he inflicts upon us. He knows the potential of what lies within us, and that is why he works so hard to shut our hearts down by emotionally handicapping us.

Our wounds and agreements are also responsible for drowning out our ability to hear Dad's voice. I have seen this several times through my kids' injuries. One particular time, I was in South Africa, where my children live, and found myself by the bedside of my daughter Mia who had contracted a serious infection inside her knee. Every three hours the nurse came by to change the dressing and each time Mia went into shock, crying and shouting from the pain. Each time I was next to her telling her how much I loved her and that it would be okay; but she could not hear a word I was saying because the pain was so much more evident than my words. The same is true when we are wounded and under unhealthy vows. Our spiritual ears and eyes are blocked by the screaming voices of our pain, false beliefs, and filters we carry within.

This discovery led me to ask, "Dad, so what are people mostly listening to—when they are wounded—that they think is Your voice, but in reality isn't?"

"Their conscience, Pablo," I heard Him reply. As I hear this, I remember the passage in Acts 10 when Peter was on Simon's roof where he has a vision, and he is told by Dad to kill and eat:

> *But he became hungry and was desiring to eat; but while they were making preparations, he fell into a trance; and he saw the sky opened up, and an object like a great sheet coming down, lowered by four*

*corners to the ground, and there were in it all kinds
of four-footed animals and crawling creatures of the
earth and birds of the air. A voice came to him, "Get
up, Peter, kill and eat!" But Peter said, "By no means,
Lord, for I have never eaten anything unholy and
unclean." Again a voice came to him a second time,
"What God has cleansed, no longer consider unholy."
This happened three times, and immediately the object
was taken up into the sky* (Acts 10:10-16 NASB).

The menu that day included items a Jew would not choose
to eat due to their religious tradition and law. Peter rightfully
declined once he had a good look at the menu, thinking this was
not the guiding voice of God within him. Yet Dad said to Peter,
"Don't call unclean what I have made clean." In other words,
Peter had to go against the voice of his conscience to do what Dad
was actually telling him to do.

It is important we understand that our conscience is not
meant to be the voice of God in our lives. If it were, then all of
us would have a different conscience, thus doing whatever we felt
like at the moment or according to the standards we've set for it.
When we choose to live this way, we are conscience driven and
not heart led. Again, I am not suggesting that we don't listen to
our conscience; but we need to understand that it is not necessarily the voice of God.

Our wounds and agreements, if we allow God to heal and
break them, can be a fantastic source of healing for others too.
This is clearly seen when Jesus meets doubting Thomas after the
resurrection. Even though Dad could have healed the wounds
on Jesus's hands and feet without leaving any scars from the
nails, He chose not to. One of the reasons He left them was so
Thomas would have hope for his own healing when he saw Jesus

and understood that though He was wounded, He had also been healed. Our scars do the same for others.

I have shared some of my biggest scars here with you, and my hope is that they will help you stop buying into the shame and the lies that tell you there is something wrong with you and that you are a loser and incomplete. The fact is that you are Dad's beloved child, and there is absolutely nothing wrong with you. You are simply wounded from living life, which means you don't need to be fixed as much as you need to be healed.

The choice is now yours: Will you ask Dad a similar question I asked all that time ago? Maybe you won't because you have been told that Dad is not interested in your wounds, and a lid needs to be put over them so you can move on. The problem is that although you try to forget and ignore the wounds you carry around, your heart doesn't.

Trying to undertake this journey with Dad with wounds and unhealthy and false beliefs is like a man with no arms and legs trying to swim across the Atlantic Ocean. The wounds and agreements in your life are not what are real and true about you. You are not what you've done or what others have done to you. You are not the sum total of your situations or the ones you have endured throughout your life. You are not your wounds or the agreements you have made. You are not where you have been or failed to reach. You are so much more than all of these things! Yet it will be very difficult for you to see this and who Dad really is until you allow Him to heal the pain and the silent hum from the agreements you have made within you.

PRAYER

God, please help me discover the agreements I have made in my life. I can now see that so much of what I have struggled with in my thoughts and life has come from the lies I bought into over the years. I want to be free. I want that small child within me to be free to grow and be the person he was always meant to be. Please help me spend time on this and not try to rush through it. I realize that this journey is long, and it takes time just like it took time to imprison me. Please keep away all the urges to try to get it right as I work through this with You. Thank You, God, for the freedom You are bringing into my life. I am deeply grateful that this is happening, no matter how late it is. Amen.

POINT OF ACTION

Review what you have been able to record in your journal during your times with God in the outdoors. Begin by focusing on one wound at a time. Ask Him to show you, as you go about your business the next few days, the ways you have been automatically misled by the agreements and false beliefs you agreed to while you were being wounded.

NOTE

1.   C.S. Lewis, *The Problem of Pain* (New York: HarperCollins, 2009), 91.

CHAPTER 7

THE REST OF US

I won't lay anything heavy or ill fitting
on you. Keep company with Me, and
you'll learn to live freely and lightly.
—JESUS

The less you know the more you believe.
—BONO

I love this program because it reminds me how much I enjoyed learning about people's behaviors in university," my wife says as we both finish watching one of her favorite programs on the National Geographic Channel, *Mind Games*. While watching a double episode of this program, I am amazed at how automatic the brain can be in the way it makes its decisions and assumptions. It is clear—from my time within the professional tennis circuit, my own journey, and now after watching this program—that the mind seeks to gain control of every situation by categorizing it and placing it into a safe and controllable box. I am also amazed at how much I have misunderstood the statement about the mind in Romans 12:2: "And do not be conformed to this world, *but be transformed by the renewing of your mind,* so that you may prove what the will of God is, that which is good and acceptable and perfect" (NASB).

So many of us have spent much time and effort focusing on this part of our being. I know I did. I worked in tennis, a sport the experts agree is 95 percent mental. They say those who are mentally tough will truly make it and go to the top echelons of the sport. Yet today, I understand that those experts' statement, like the one Paul made in Romans, is only part of the truth because it is missing one big ingredient, which we discover as we process this truth with our hearts and not just our clever intellects.

During my years of playing and then coaching tennis for some of the top players in the world, I realized how flawed an approach is when it is based only on various concentration and controlling mechanisms, when it comes to trying to control our mind and life through them. Each time I worked through these techniques to help a player successfully bring his or her mind under control, something out of their control would happen that would cause it to go into overdrive. Repeatedly, this would take place with my players and then with me when I watched them play.

For years I struggled along, trying to bargain with my mind to bring it under control. Dad only knows how many millions of units of emotional energy I must have spent trying to stay on top of it. No matter how hard I tried, however, this approach always led me to a place where the total loss of control and breakdowns were familiar. Once the player or I found ourselves in this space of chaos, neither one of us was able to function any longer at the level previously attained as we began to go up and down like a yo-yo.

This scenario also repeated itself outside the tennis court, like when we sat down to discuss a strategy before a match in which a player was going against an opponent who was superior to them on paper. Each time, the mind collapsed when it was unable to find the answers it felt comfortable with in order to feel in control. It goes without saying that this led my players and me to feel weak and tired, as we were continuously defeated by invisible foes that didn't really have to do very much to throw us off course.

Dad showed me something that not only changed my approach to coaching, but also my approach as a whole to life and my relationship with Him. One morning, at one of the tournaments I attended as a coach, I was walking by the beach, and Dad asked me, "Why are you trying to control everything?"

This question completely threw me. What was that supposed to mean? Aren't we supposed to work hard and try to cover our bases as best we can so that we can hopefully get the results we think we need, in order that life can go as best as it possibly can? Isn't this what Paul meant when he told us that we needed to have our mind transformed?

"So, how are you planning on transforming your mind, Pablo?" Dad asks.

"Well, you work hard to memorize Scripture, and then you meditate on certain verses, and then little by little your mind and life are transformed, I guess," I replied.

"And how is that working for you, Pablo?" Dad asks.

"Well, it is frickin' hard, but I think I am making progress," I reply.

Next, Dad asks me a question that finally throws me overboard. "And what about your players? They don't memorize Scripture, so how is their mind going to be transformed?"

The answer I think about is pitiful as I realize I am trying to be like Job and have a go at pretending I am as clever as God.

"Okay, You win again," I say. "What do I need to understand from this?" I ask in an almost defeated and sarcastic manner.

"That's the point, Pablo. Your mind thinks it has to either win or lose. You are using your mind to achieve a specific result. This result is what you focus on because you think it will somehow add value and improve your life. You believe the illusion that it will take you one step closer to that place where you think you will find happiness and peace," He replies. "The problem is that this way of manipulating your life through your mind means you limit your life to what you know, can remember, and are able to do." He further says, "This approach of yours is not what it means to have your mind transformed. This approach of yours means using the mind for something it was not designed to be used for."

As I hear Dad whisper this last statement, I now see that what actually needs to happen to the mind is that it needs to get out of the way when it comes to matters that belong to the heart. It is just not able to process or even understand what the heart can. When we live an integrated life, the ongoing chatter within our minds quiets down. As this happens, the mind takes its rightful place where it no longer gets in the way of the heart flowing in and through our life. The mind is a brilliant part of us, and so is our ability to reason. We need to use our minds. However, this needs to be done in its rightful place and for the purpose it was created.

The mind is where the ego resides. And I think we can all agree that our ego loves to sit on the throne. It does not like to be left aside, nor does it like to feel out of control. This is where the false illusion of feeling in control originates. The ego is also the very thing that limits our lives, because it leads us to believe that if we somehow can figure it all out, then we can control enough of life so it can deliver the result we believe we need or deserve.

> The problem is that while this game is played, we totally miss the fact that the cross was meant to open the way for us to see that a relationship was and had been available to us all along.

Take this assumption and apply it to your relationship with Dad. How do you even begin to understand with your mind truths like everything seen and unseen is contained within Dad? How are you able to understand that Dad is everywhere and knows everything—like He is now in Tel Aviv while I write this, and He is also with my friends in Pennsylvania while they sleep? How do you have faith and believe with your mind? Is faith a formula that we figure out? How do we relate from our mind with a God who is wild and free? How do we remain open to spontaneity in our lives and invite the element of mystery in if we need to always feel in control of everything around us and within us? How are we able to understand that we are already living in eternity, and that within our heart we are eternal? Better yet, how do we surpass the barrier in our mind that just because our body is within reality does not mean our heart and life has to be limited by it?

The sad thing is that if you go to Amazon.com, there are thousands of books that will tell you of a way that most of the above questions, if not all of them, can be figured out through clever thinking. Therefore, we can have even greater control of our life by controlling what God gives us and when He gives it to us.

The problem is that while this game is played, we totally miss the fact that the cross was meant to open the way for us to see

127

that a relationship was and has been available to us all along. The cross was not meant for us to start a new religion based on what we can and cannot do through control. When we live from our mind alone, we always have the need to explain our lives instead of being free enough to express them.

We take things like the Bible and make it our main source of sustenance primarily because we can touch it, read it, and, with a certain amount of skill, we can get it to say whatever we want. Yet little do we realize that when we make the Bible our main source of sustenance, and not God within our heart, it is the same as us eating a menu and not the food it tells us about. Remember, the only reason the Bible comes alive is because we know God and not the other way around.

When we play this game called religion, where we wrongfully use our mind to relate with God, we are unfortunately led to a place where we cut out the very nature of God from our lives as we pursue a false holiness, which will only be responsible for delivering more holes in our heart. We need to see and understand the errors that the wrongful use of our mind leads us to make when we are led to link our significance with our inconsistent performance. I know only too well how this trap works, blinding us to the fact that our significance can only come from one place—the oneness we have with Dad.

Plain and simple, we need to grasp the fact that the wrongful use of our mind will always lead us to a place where we seek to live a results-orientated life, hence, the reason for our overpowering need to control. Every time we choose to do this, we are blinded from seeing that our faith is no longer in God but in the systems we are using. These clever systems are also responsible for hiding from us the truth—the same happiness and peace we try to force God to give us through systems is already within us.

Like my players and I did in the past, if this is how we attempt to journey on our spiritual walk, we will always be limited by what others tell us, what we read, and what we know. Although in some cases this can be quite diverse, this will only mean we will need to spend more time remembering these things than playing the game or walking the walk that is before us.

> When we live from our mind alone, we always have the need to explain our lives instead of being free enough to express them.

Transforming our mind according to Romans 12:2 means changing the way we approach life and how we use our mind in that approach. It is clear we have been given a mind and a body to be able to function in this world. They are like a set of tools given to help us complete a certain task. The problem arises when we use these tools to do the work for which another set of tools is responsible.

When we use our mind to do what only the heart can do, it is the same as trying to use a spoon to cut down a 100-year-old oak tree. Yes, I know some of you might eventually get the job done, even if it's the only job you ever do; however, why use a spoon when you have a chainsaw available? The way we choose to approach this walk of ours makes it so much harder than it was actually meant to be.

Have you ever considered the difference between the two approaches?

- Our mind tells us that life is about us needing to figure it out by getting as much information and knowledge as possible; our heart tells us that we need to discover what is already within us.

- Our mind tells us that we need to stay in control; our heart invites us to trust and have faith in the One who lives within as we release the control of our lives.

- Our mind drives us to build our own salvation plan by trying to get it right every time. Our heart shows us that the Kingdom of heaven is already within us and we just need to wake up to be able to see it.

- Our mind drives us to control and hold every-thing tight in our lives. Our heart encourages us to loosen our grip so that we can discover and receive something new each day.

This is what Jesus was essentially saying to Nicodemus in John 3:5-6:

> *You're not listening. Let me say it again. Unless a person submits to this original creation—the "wind-hovering-over-the-water" creation, the invisible moving the visible, a baptism into a new life—it's not possible to enter God's kingdom. When you look at a baby, it's just that: a body you can look at and touch. But the person who takes shape within is formed by something you can't see and touch—the Spirit—and becomes a living spirit.*

And Paul was telling the Corinthians much the same thing:

That is what the Scriptures mean when they say, "No eye has seen, no ear has heard, and no mind has imagined what God has prepared for those who love him" (1 Corinthians 2:9 NLT).

As far as the mind is concerned, if we are already like God, then the mind does not like this because it has nothing to toil toward. The mind then loses its place of control in the journey because it can't attach itself to anything, because we are already whole and complete in Dad. We have everything we need—we lack nothing in Him.

Please don't misunderstand me here. I am all for hard work and doing your best; however, when you begin to place your faith and ability to see on these two things alone, then you are trusting what you can do and the results you can achieve, instead of trusting the One who dwells within you. Every result we achieve in life belongs to Dad. Our role is to enjoy the journey as we remain present with Him in each moment of every day. This is why the ego is always concerned with heaven and hell, where we'll be in the future, and not with the here and now, as our heart and spirit are.

Even though I have discovered much of this over time, no experience was as powerful as a ride I took back to the airport in Johannesburg after seeing my kids in South Africa. During this hour drive, Dad opened my eyes to show me how the ego works through the mind. This revelation brought clarity, understanding, and freedom to me and to the players with whom I worked.

I will never forget that all I had available to me was in the present. My ego within my mind had always led me to believe that if I thought about the future and all it could throw at me, I would then be able to better prepare for it. Yet, as good and wise as that might sound, as I did this I traded it in for the only thing I had, which was the present—what was taking place right in front of me.

The mind, in the name of results, will not only convince us that we can create a future that will be good enough to redeem the past we are so ashamed of, but it will also prevent us from owning the past we have had and the consequences and impact it had on our hearts, because it leads us to run away from it instead of facing it. This is exactly the illusion Adam and Eve brought with them when they were driven out of the reality of the Garden. They shifted their focus from the heart to the body and the mind. The mind became the self-imposed king, and the heart took a back seat as they welcomed a new reality where the main focus became the building of a false identity through the results they accomplished in order to replace the one they thought they had lost.

In order to have a role in our lives, the mind also requires a problem or a situation that it needs to bring under control. For example, if you have ever paused in your life to take a look at a sunset, did you find yourself scared or worried when you did it? Or when you are sharing an intimate moment with your spouse, are you worried or anxious? The truth is that if you are worried, fearful, or anxious, you cannot fully enjoy, appreciate, or actively participate in either of these two events. The only way for us to enjoy and participate in such life-enriching events is for us to be fully present and in the moment. I wonder how much our inability to take the time to fully enjoy these experiences and other precious moments in our journey are because of our choosing to live mainly from our mind.

It is funny how we often blame our suffering and shortcomings on God shortchanging us. But do we still believe that it is God who is responsible for our suffering? The fact is that much of what we suffer comes down to the wrongful use of our mind, and the way it leads us to approach this journey we're on. We need to remember that our mind was designed to remember facts like the name of a person, an address, an appointment we have tomorrow at 9 a.m. with the dentist, and maybe the birthday of a loved one. Yet, if we are honest about our approach to life and the way we overload and misuse our mind, it means that our mind is not able to perform the task it was designed for. If you don't believe me, check your smartphone and see how many reminders and alarms you have programmed to remind you of everything you need to do in the upcoming days, including the birthday of a loved one or even your wedding anniversary.

And the same is true about the heart trying to fill the role that the mind has been assigned. Imagine trying to remember someone's name with your heart or information about your profession or career. The fact is that you won't be able to do this, as the heart was never designed for this purpose. Have you ever wondered why is it that we can accept that the heart is not able to do this, yet we find it so hard to accept the reverse scenario?

The reality is that the ego within our mind leads us away from our heart because it aims to take over the role that only the heart can fulfill, and it does so at the expense of itself. The minute we learn to loosen our grip around the results of our lives and the future we so desperately need to control, is the minute we begin to transfer the command post of our lives from our ego to our heart.

I will never forget the first time one of my tennis players was able to play a whole match from this place. I asked her how it felt, and she said, "Well, it was amazing. I didn't feel the need to think about what would happen if I lost this point or how I would be three-zero down instead of two-one." Clearly, her focus had transferred from trying to control and manipulate a future that had not happened to enjoying what was right in front of her.

When I asked her to describe what was going on within her mind, the answer was amazing. She replied, "Absolute stillness." I smile every time I remember this because it brings to mind Psalm 46:10, where Dad tells us, "Loosen your grip over your mind that you may be able to understand me with your heart" (Pablo's paraphrase).

Isn't it troublesome that when we have what we call a quiet time, we are anything but quiet? Our driven egotistical mind is persistent to the point where we can't even have a quiet moment with God or even rest at night. Like a continual beating of a drum, it goes on and on adding to the yoke we already carry, without ever being able to find real rest.

But Jesus asks us,

> *"Are you tired? Worn out? Burned out on religion? Come to me. Get away with me and you'll recover your life. I'll show you how to take a real rest. Walk with me and work with me—watch how I do it. Learn the unforced rhythms of grace.* **I won't lay anything heavy or ill-fitting on you. Keep company with me and you'll learn to live freely and lightly"** (Matthew 11:28-30).

Now either Jesus was abusing and lying to us, or He knew of a different way to live.

It is interesting to see that the only people Jesus took up an issue with were the religious leaders of His time. He didn't have a problem with the Torah, the commandments, the sinners who surrounded Him, or even their sin. This was because He saw the way the religious leaders approached their walk with God, and their life as a whole was nothing more than an eternal and never-ending task that led nowhere. He accused them of traveling halfway around the world to get one convert and make him more a son of the devil than he ever was before they indoctrinated him with a journey in which working and trying harder was king.

This is also the reason why the wrongful use of the mind leads us to a place where we are unable to accept the grace of God. Grace is simply saying, "It is okay to relax. Don't worry about the future. Don't worry about everything that is wrong or dirty. It is okay. I got you. Enjoy my love and me in this moment you have. There is no need to fret and charge around trying to make it work or get it right. All is well within you. The Kingdom and King you seek so hard after and that you try to build and understand are already within your heart. Loosen your grip and be still. Focus on what I am doing right now, and tomorrow will take care of itself."

The religious approach, however, has no time, nor does it like or embrace grace as part of its doctrine. Yes, it can't deny that we are awakening by grace; however, it has a hard time accepting that we remain awake by grace. Just like in tennis, we are not called to play in order to win or lose as much as we are called to play with our whole heart—never considering what may or may not happen if we hit the ball hard or soft, but simply following our heart and the purposes that reason knows nothing about.

Living from the heart also leads us into a place where we learn to embrace mystery and faith. We suddenly become able to take the next step without having a guaranteed result or the need to know what the outcome will be. And yes, I know you are thinking, "But what about the commandments, and what about our behavior modification?"

Well, like the tennis players I work with, the minute we remove our focus from trying to get a certain result we think will deliver us the grand prize of holiness and happiness, is the moment we enter into a space where this responsibility falls on Dad and the reality within our hearts. This heavy yoke of having to get it right disappears, and we are suddenly able to embrace God and ourselves fully.

As we do this, we start to enter into a reality where healing becomes possible and the light yoke Jesus spoke about becomes a real experience. When this happens, our heart comes alive and with it a new ability to understand and see what we have never been able to see before. Always remember it is not the knowledge that you accumulate in your mind that changes you; it is the understanding that surfaces from your new heart. Your mind was never designed to understand or have the ability to grasp the eternal things of God. (See First Corinthians 2:14.)

We need to allow Dad to deliver us from the god we have built in our minds. We need to loosen our grip around this and the things that have gone alongside it, so that in their place new life can flow. This is what proper rest is all about. This is what Jesus spoke about, and the only way we will ever enter into it is by laying down our lives (our attempts through our egotistical mind), so we may be able to find our true identities that are contained within our heart.

Our incessant attempt to figure it all out through the wrong use of our mind drives our focus away from all that is beautiful and true about us. The egotistical mind works in great partnership with our body. In our flesh, our ego has found a willing and sound ally. I don't have to go into great detail about the shame and disgust so many of us feel every time we are reminded that we don't look like a perfect 10 or like the model on the billboard we just drove by. This false reality is so polluted by the lie that tells us that if we have a strong and fit body, then we will have a strong mind, which means we will have a successful and healthy life.

Take a look at how well Jesus addressed this when He spoke to the Pharisees in Matthew 23:27-28:

> *You're hopeless, you religion scholars and Pharisees! Frauds! You're like manicured grave plots, grass clipped and the flowers bright, but six feet down it's all rotting bones and worm-eaten flesh. People look at you and think you're saints, but beneath the skin you're total frauds.*

What Jesus was hitting on is not the fact that it is wrong to be fit or look good. Neither is it wrong to dress well, be well groomed, and presentable. No, what Jesus was driving at was that when these things are what we focus on, then we do this at the expense of what really matters, which is the condition of our heart. Our real identity is not found in what we do, become, achieve, how much we make, or what we wear or look like. Our real identity is found within our heart.

It doesn't matter how much money we give, how much we do for others, or how many times we pray or read the Bible. If our aim is driven by a mindset of performance in order to transform our lives into a perfect mirage, then we will miss the Kingdom and the God of that Kingdom who is within us. In fact, I am convinced more than ever that this is what Paul meant in Romans 8:5-8 when he told us:

> *Those who think they can do it on their own end up obsessed with measuring their own moral muscle but never get around to exercising it in real life. Those who trust God's action in them find that God's Spirit is in them—living and breathing God! Obsession with self in these matters is a dead end; attention to God leads us out into the open, into a spacious, free life. Focusing on the self is the opposite of focusing on God. Anyone completely absorbed in self ignores God, ends up thinking more about self than God. That person ignores who God is and what he is doing. And God isn't pleased at being ignored.*

We are not called to live from our mind alone, but rather from our heart. If we live from the mind, then it will be all about our self-preservation. Our false self is king. Here we look after one and only one person, and that is our false self, which is created by our ego and is supported by our flesh. In this place dualism thrives and we are led to believe the illusion of separation, which then drives us to create a false reality outside of ourselves where we try to replicate what we had back in the Garden. Yet sadly, as we try to bridge this illusionary gap, we actually lead ourselves further from the truth rather than closer to it.

The approach of using the body led by the ego is what leads many of us to fall into unhealthy addictions. Our flesh develops impulses and compulsions that have the potential to become addictions if they are given enough time. These addictions lead us to the belief that they are the only way to find peace and satisfaction, which gives us a sense of control. When this happens, our focus is then fixed on satisfying the flesh instead of pursuing a life from the heart. This approach means we are led to live out of our flesh and not our heart.

This way of intellectually approaching our journey with God is the primary reason for the disintegration of our beings. If you don't believe me, check out these statistics by the Schaeffer Institute that speak of those we all think know best.

After 18 years of researching pastoral trends, here are some of the results. Seventy percent of pastors constantly fight depression, and seventy-one percent are burned out. Seventy-two percent of pastors confess to only studying the Bible when they need to prepare for a sermon. Eighty percent believe that their involvement in pastoral ministry has negatively affected their family life, and seventy percent say that they don't have a close friend they can be open and honest with.[1]

Please take a minute to reflect on these eye-opening results.

This is why Jesus was inviting us to re-center our being. Before we are believers, our souls feed themselves through worldly lusts and pleasures. The needs and desires our souls experience are met with the greatest efficiency possible, which explains all the addictions and troubles we experience before we see Jesus. This approach is acting in accordance with the dualistic system that is prevalent in the world.

As awakened believers, our souls are fed through the heart. Our spirit, along with the Holy Spirit, filters how we are fed, and it is through living centered in our heart that we fulfill our desires in the way God has planned. Remember, our heart contains desires, needs, and wants within it, while impulses, compulsions, and addictions belong to the flesh. We are led to the latter by the degeneration that takes place in our lives as we attempt to do life only through our dualistic minds and not through our heart.

Addictions are not just drugs, porn, or alcohol either; religion can also become an addiction.

I wonder what you are pursuing in your life today. Are you focusing on working hard to perfect your theology and behavior in order to get it right so God can love you and bless you and somehow embrace you? Or are you simply walking into the reality of the Kingdom and the embrace of the King within it, which has actually been there all along? My religion was an addiction for many years as I tried hard to use it to feed my soul. Again and again, I aimed to use religion as a tool to control my life, others, and even God Himself. Yet, like all addictions, what started as a tool to help me control the pain and suffering in my life, ended up controlling me.

Re-centering our beings is not an easy journey, and neither is it pretty. It is scary to let go of what we have used for so long as a crutch. Will we stand or will we fall? Will it be okay or will it be lost? Will we find the narrow way or will we remain stuck in the wide path? What about the God I believed in and thought I had figured out? What will happen to Him?

These are all valid questions I have had to face and still do at times. As we release the god of our mind, we will be led to travel through spaces where we feel like atheists. What we believed will start fading and eventually be gone and, in its place, we will feel a void. These voids are hard to travel through, like David spoke about in Psalm 23 when he referred to us traveling through the valley of death. Yet I can tell you with all certainty that as difficult as these experiences are, what surfaces into the place that was once occupied by the false self is nothing short of miraculous and transforming.

Just like when my players reached an unprecedented place in their careers after they finally trusted enough to start playing from their hearts and not only from their minds, I too have begun to come each day into a new reality and understanding of Dad and myself that is hard for me to explain through words because, perhaps, words are not meant to be able to explain it in its entirety. I will never forget the day the god of my mind was dissolved and loosened from my life and the sudden freedom and awakening that replaced it.

You are presented with the same choice each day of your journey. You can either stay in the certainty of your illusion that is anchored to the shores of familiarity, or you can take a risk and venture out into the unfamiliar and the unknown where there will be no more limits as you come into the abundant life Jesus said He came to bring. Yes, faith and trust are required to take this step, but then again, didn't someone say long ago that through faith He would be pleased? (See Hebrews 11:6.)

PRAYER

God, I feel so lost and I am thinking, "Now what?" How is it possible that I have tried for so long, and even believed that I could somehow work all this out through my clever thinking? Now I see why it has been hard to have faith or even love those who are hard to love. I was trying to do it with my mind instead of my heart. Please help me to make this transition in my life as I transfer the throne room from my mind to my heart. Help me to understand the difference between using my mind to manipulate and control and letting my heart lead me. Slowly, I am beginning to see how foolish we are when we believe that what is going on inside our mind is that You and I are relating with each other. Please help me let go of this approach and loosen my grip around the god that my mind has become so I can allow You, God, to lead me from within my heart. Amen.

POINT OF ACTION

Take one situation in your life where you have always used your mind to decide what to do. Take your journal and make two lists of ten items each. On the first list, think hard about the pros and write them down. On the other list, try to think even harder as you write down the cons. Once you have finished this, sit back on a comfortable chair. As you become still, ask your heart what decision you need to make. Write down how the two experiences were different. Write down things like how you felt, which one was harder to come up with, and whether you reached the same decision in your heart as you did with your mind, etc.

NOTE

1.   Richard J. Krejcir, "Statistics on Pastors," Into Thy Word, 2007, accessed September 30, 2014, http://www.intothyword.org/apps/articles/default.asp?articleid=36562.

CHAPTER 8

NOW

I AM who I AM.
—God

The distinction between the past, present and future is only a stubbornly persistent illusion.
—Albert Einstein

W
e are finally here," says our host in Medellin, Colombia, as we arrive at the hotel where my wife and I will be spending the next two days. We have just spent more than an hour working our way through the manic traffic of this beautiful city. My host, who is driving and sitting next to his wife, gets out of the car to open the trunk, where we proceed to get our luggage. The hotel porter has come out to welcome us.

It sure feels good to be back here again. I have visited this city many times before for business. Not only is it a beautiful place, but the people here are some of the most positive and happy people I have ever met. During the flight, I told Madeleine how wonderful Medellin is and how much I was looking forward to her experiencing it with me.

We are standing around the car while the porter takes my hand luggage into the hotel lobby and motions that he will return for the bigger pieces still inside the open trunk. Suddenly, out of nowhere, I am pushed away from the car by two armed men. They had followed us all the way from the airport in order to rob us.

"What are you looking at, you @#$! $# @ @#$%&?" the man with the gun shouts at me in Spanish while he points a .38 revolver right at my face.

"Relax, my friend," I tell him as calm as day. "You can have whatever you want."

"What are you so relaxed about, you @#$%? I am going to #@$% kill you before I take everything you have!" he replies in a very loud voice. As I look around, I see my wife, who is by now on the other side of the car, with a look of fear on her face. Our hosts are also paralyzed and so is a small child who is clinging to his mom's leg not far away. The hotel porter has realized what is happening outside, so he doesn't return. I am the only one who is actually engaging the thieves because everyone else is too stunned to do so.

"Why are you going to do that?" I reply. "You know we are tourists, and if you kill us you will be caught because our government will make sure of that. So just take what you want." As all this is going on, I am experiencing an amazing peace and stillness within and around me. Such is the stillness and awareness in me that at one point, when the thief turns and aims the gun at my host, I start to think about kicking him on the wrist to loosen the gun from his hand, so we can stop him from taking everything we have. As I consider this, however, he points the gun back at me.

"Give me your chain and your watch, you @#$%!" he screams at me.

"Yep, no problem," I say as I begin to remove them while looking straight into his eyes. I can see the fear that is in him and how nervous he and his partner are. Once they have taken everything, they begin to run away as we all take cover inside the hotel.

Our host takes us down to the police station where we file a report. The police officer asks us to recount the incident, which we all describe to a T. I can see from the officer's face that he is amazed at the outcome of this situation. "You know, first of all," the officer says, "I am very sorry for what has happened to you here in our city today. Second, I think you need to know that what normally happens when locals or even tourists are robbed is that they are first killed and then the thieves take whatever they can. They do this so no one can identify them.

"Sir, I believe what saved you today was how calm you remained and how you engaged the thieves," the officer continues. "Normally, people panic and begin to scream or try to flee the situation, so they are shot. What you did was unbelievable. It literally saved your life. How did you manage that?"

"I stayed in the moment, felt the peace and protection of God within me, and knew we were going to be okay," I reply. He simply stares at me, speechless.

When we enter into the domain of our heart, one of the dimensions we begin to experience on a frequent basis is the absence of panic and anxiety as we become fully present in the moment we have before us, no matter what is going on. How different I would have reacted to this event in Colombia had it happened ten years earlier. The truth is that I lived and approached my life in a way that was the complete opposite to how I chose to respond this day in Medellin.

From the moment I opened my eyes in the morning until the moment I closed them at night, all my days were filled with thoughts about the past and how I could redeem it by trying to manipulate, force, and control a future that had not yet happened. Worry, anxiety, and fear were always with me. Never was there a time when they were not close to me, so I couldn't rest from this thought that continually reminded me that I still had not made it in life. The presence of these foes meant that hours turned into days, days into weeks, weeks into months, and months into years without me even noticing that all along time was slipping away.

The reality is that if I had not been present in that moment in Colombia, you would probably not be reading this book. What happened that day reaffirmed to me that living in the present was not just some far-removed eastern religious concept, but was indeed how Jesus chose to live and how we will live as we begin to do life from our heart. It also showed me how remaining in the present better prepares us for the future that has not yet arrived.

If we continue to live only from our mind, then we will eventually end up buying into an unhealthy perspective of life that limits and causes us to respond erratically when things don't work the way we believe they should. The reality of the world we live in is that we see everything with a beginning and an end. This point of view leads us to set deadlines and time limits, prepare forecasts, and even make plans with goals that need to be achieved by a certain time. This way, we are led to believe the false illusion that we can control when things happen, even though we know things don't always work this way.

> Unfortunately, our need to control has led many of
> us to discount this way of living because we have
> believed the lie that if we enjoy and fully experience
> the moment we are in, then we will not be able to
> arrive at the future as best prepared as possible.

There is nothing wrong with planning or goal setting as long as we don't remain with our eyes fixed on the fulfillment of the goal, or worse yet, we spend today focusing on tomorrow, trying to figure out how and what we can do in the days to come so we can fulfill a goal. When we do this, we develop the mentality that leads us to believe there are sell-by dates in our lives by which we have to get something right, otherwise we may be discarded or time will simply run out. This approach, unfortunately, is the same one we take in our walk with Dad.

When this happens, we find ourselves spending most of our time comparing ourselves with others who are getting what we are not, or seeing what Dad seems to be doing through them that He is not doing through us. This leads to insecurity and the need to try harder, as we assume that we must be doing something wrong because we are not making the same progress we believe others are making. We, of course, assume this because we are clearly not able to see what is actually going on inside other people.

As we get older, we grow desperate in the name of "what do we have to show for our lives" without realizing that the reason why it appears to be "not much" is because we have been mostly absent from the only time and space where life can be affected and impacted, which is the now—the present.

Unfortunately, our need to control has led many of us to discount this way of living because we have believed the lie that if we enjoy and fully experience the moment we are in, then we will not be able to arrive at the future as best prepared as possible. This, at face value, sounds right. However, let me share with you what Dad showed me that day in Colombia, and also what He taught me through the Scriptures. Not only does it negate this lie, but it also exposes it for what it truly is—the need to be in control of our destiny.

I find myself inside another airplane traveling back to Israel after a few weeks away. Opening my Bible, I stumble upon the story of Jairus and his dying daughter in Luke 8, a story I have read a number of times. Reading about the woman who had been bleeding for 12 years, who most believe is the main feature and message behind this story, I feel Dad nudge me to stay on this passage. "I want to show you something, Pablo, that will help you see how living in the present is the best way to prepare yourself for the future," Dad whispers.

In Luke 8:40, Jesus arrives in the area, and as people see Him, they naturally run toward Him to welcome Him. While this is happening, Jairus approaches and falls at Jesus's feet, begging Him to please come and heal his dying daughter.

Jesus, being fully present and aware, probably looks at Jairus, realizing he is acting out of desperation. Jesus realizes he does not have the faith to see this miracle, so He understands—between Him agreeing to come and them arriving at the house where the little girl is being kept—something needs to happen in order to activate faith within Jairus's heart. Jesus, being the amazing and loving man that He is, figures a way to change all this so that when they arrive at the house Jairus will have the necessary faith to receive the miracle.

As they begin to walk through the crowd, Jesus gets separated from Jairus (I believe on purpose), as Jesus knows that what needs to happen to activate Jairus's faith is going to happen within the crowd. We all know what happens next from what we read. However, have we ever considered what was happening with Jairus when the woman with the issue of blood is pressing in to Jesus?

Being the leader of the local synagogue, Jairus would have known who this woman was. He would have probably prayed with her many times, together with the other Pharisees in the area, for her healing. He would have probably sent her to see some of the best doctors in town. In other words, he would have been fully aware of the impossible condition this woman had been carrying for more than a decade, which meant, as far as he was concerned, she was beyond any possible cure.

Suddenly, as he is walking and maybe wondering how insensitive Jesus is by taking a pit stop along the way to healing his daughter, he stops as he realizes what is going on around him. He is so taken aback by what he is witnessing that he calms down completely and, in fact, he even forgets that his daughter is dying. We see in Luke 8:49 that someone has to actually come and find him to tell him that his daughter has now died.

Jesus is still within the crowd. There would have been a lot of noise; dust would have been kicked up, children were probably screaming, women wailing at the miracle just performed. Yet Jesus is able to hear what someone says to Jairus in the distance and responds, "Do not be afraid any longer; only believe, and she will be made well" (Luke 8:50 NASB).

All along Jesus was fully aware of Jairus, and what He had just done was to ignite the faith that would overtake the fear that had clearly captured him earlier. The truth is that within the words of Jairus's servant telling him that his daughter was now dead was the potential to kill faith. The little girl was probably dead; however, Jesus had Jairus's attention because he was fully present with Him in the moment.

As Jesus speaks and tells him not to listen but to believe, what He is actually saying to Jairus is, "Stay with Me, right here, right now. I am doing something that if you remain present with Me and not try to run ahead, it will activate something within you that will give you the desire of your heart when we arrive at your house. Don't worry about what the servant has just said or what it may or may not look like outwardly, just stay with Me right here, Jairus."

When they finally arrived at the house, Jesus did not allow anyone to enter the house with Him except Peter, John, James, and the parents of the little girl. Again, this is a great clue that shows us that only those Jesus knew were present and had the faith to see her healed were allowed in.

As I finish reading this passage of Scripture, I put my Bible down on my lap and turn my gaze toward the horizon outside the plane's window. "Wow!" I think. "How is it that I was never able to see this before?" If that woman were not healed, Jairus would have lost his daughter. As I sit there, I see in Jairus, while he remains present with Jesus, the same stillness and peace rise up within him that enabled me not to panic, though my life hung in the balance in Colombia. "What is this? What is actually happening that two human beings are suddenly able to somehow bypass the commotion and emotions that dominate us when we are under pressure in life?" I ask.

As I sit there, I begin to understand that when we are present, we are completely surrendered to God within us and not the ego within our minds. Results and consequences take a back seat and lose their importance because it is no longer about us or what is happening right in front of us. We enter into the reality of our heart and the One who is more real than anyone we can see. When here, we are enabled to be fully aware of what is being given to us within instead of panicking to get whatever we can to fix and change what is happening to us.

Think of Jesus with a crown of thorns, knowing full well who He is, being accused of something He has not done and that is simply not true. Yet He remains quiet and is even able to answer Pilate's questions that are important for Him to answer, which pertain mainly to who He really is. Again, no panic, no anxiety, no need to run—a fully surrendered individual who has not submitted to the fear and anxiety that began to plague Him in the garden hours earlier.

When we live in the present, we are able to understand that what hits our eye is not really what is going on. There is another world and reality that we are unable to see with the eyes of the flesh. This is because our natural eyes that feed information to our minds are not designed to be able to see this, because they are only a lens. The only eyes that can see this are the eyes of our heart, as these are used as projectors that allow us to see from within what is really going on. The eyes of our heart can only be used to observe when we are present and still within.[1]

The wrongful way we allow our mind to run the show is the reason most of us live absent lives and miss the real story that is happening around us. In order for us to understand how this works, it is necessary for us to understand how the mind works. I mentioned in an earlier chapter how the mind was designed to remember things like appointments, directions to go somewhere, and so on. However, the problem begins when the mind is used to try to figure a way out from what is happening in front of us—the present. Allow me to explain.

In order for the mind to work, it requires an event to trigger it. Events are only found in the past or in the future. In the moment there are no events, only what is happening right now. For example, let's say I check my bank account every day because I am worried that I am not going to make it through the end of the month. While I am doing this, I am remembering how close and nasty it was last month, which then invites fear. Suddenly, I shift toward the future and think about what else I can do that might make a difference in my situation, which then activates more worry and anxiety. I begin to think about whom I may call or what I may do. As I do this, my desperation grows and my condition worsens. Yet all along I fail to see the email notice that has just popped up on the corner of my screen announcing that I have received a work offer.

I log off my computer and go down to the pub to meet a friend. There I talk it over with him, and with every word I get more scared as I realize I have no way of making this work. I begin to think that I can't even pay for the beer I just ordered. So I return home. That night, my mind is actually aching from all the thinking I have done. I have just spent a whole day being completely absent because I have continued to look for the answer to my situation outside of me.

Before going to bed, I open my computer to check my email. Bang! There it is—a job offer that will see me through until the end of the month. Amazed, I realize this email is the third one they have sent me because I have obviously missed it twice before while I was running around desperately trying to fix my life instead of discovering it.

Imagine that instead of wasting all that brain activity, I would have chosen not to worry and remain present. Imagine what other things I probably missed along the way that Dad would have sent to help me, yet I either didn't notice them or discarded them as non-starters because to the eyes of my ego they didn't look the way a good opportunity should. Jesus clearly told us in Matthew 6 not to worry about tomorrow because all that worry does is drive us to try to find the answer somewhere else, while failing to notice that the answer is within us all along.

God sees life and time differently than we do. Most of our panic, fear, and anxiety come from our inability to see the bigger picture we are a part of. This laser focus means we can't take a step back to see past the penny fear and anxiety are leading us to hold in front of our eyes.

God is not in a hurry with His plan and purpose, though we often are. People in Bible times saw time as seasons and not as days, weeks, and months. Yes, they lived by days, weeks, and months too, but when it came to the overall theme of life, they saw it in seasons.[2] A season is something we cannot control with our minds. In our heart, on the other hand, where we can see things from an eternal perspective, we understand that seasons are actually healthy and productive because a person is able to freely live each moment with purpose and understanding, not worrying about when it may or may not come to an end, or what may or may not happen.

Dad decides these things while we enjoy the journey and what is right before us. It sounds too easy to be true and somewhat irresponsible; however, if we study the life of Jesus and the words of God throughout history, we will see a distinct air of peace and calmness in everything they did and said. They have always known that there is nothing wrong or anything that needs to be fixed by a certain date or time.

Our heart is connected to a completely different time zone. The only way we can live a life that is not constantly plagued by worry and anxiety is by living in the present. In the moment, there is nothing to worry about, there is nothing to fear, and there is nothing to be anxious about. These things can only draw the energy they need to exist from the events that happened in the past or the ones they think will be happening in the future. Living from the heart is not something we can enter through effort and manipulation, but rather something we step into by accepting the same grace, love, and truth that are responsible for sustaining this timeless reality.

This is nothing new. This syndrome began in the Garden of Eden when the illusion of separation was purchased. Since then, we have left the reality of the heart and have begun to construct another reality through our minds, which functions through fear, worry, and anxiety, which are responsible for all the stress that leads to many of the sicknesses we face in the world today.

I realize you are probably saying, "Well, it is easy for you, Pablo, to say this as you don't understand or have the pressures I have in my life." Well, let me tell you I know pressure better than most. Remember, I lived and worked many years in an environment where results were king. I was always judged on whether I won or lost—no in between. One week I was popular because the player I coached won a big tournament. The next week I was nothing because my player lost in the first round of another tournament.

Thousands, if not millions, on TV often witnessed my work. The experts and the media were always on standby and ready to give their verdict of what they thought was an extension of the work of my hands. Talk about the potential for a yo-yo ride. Yet the more I focused on enjoying the moment and the season, the more successful I became.

Living in the present is no guarantee of circumstantial success; however, it will set you in a space where you will know that no matter what happens, you are loved and embraced by the One who loves you like no one else can. Your life and your relationships will be richer and fuller. Your priorities will change as you align yourself with this newfound reality where you focus on what is important and not urgent.

In this space, you will be able to allow your life to become the journey of discovery it was always meant to be, and you will cease from your attempts to try to fix it. There is a reason why when Dad met Moses, He didn't call Himself the great I *was* or the great I *will*, but instead the great I AM. This timeless, great I AM is the same One who lives and is one with us. He is present with us each moment of our life, even if we are not.

Today, I realize most of the problems and suffering I have experienced in my life could have been avoided if I had stopped long enough to be still and present in the situation. This way, I would have had a chance to see and understand that all the doing and getting I thought would fix my life was, in fact, responsible for breaking it down even more. Our spiritual journey is the moment we have in front of us—not the one that just was or the one that may or may not come next. All we can do is respond to the situation before us without resistance and as we are required, because any other approach will be based on our obsession to control and manipulate what we don't yet have.

We can't see, hear, or even feel Dad's presence in our lives when we are absent. In the moment, it is far easier to loosen the grip around the need to control our lives and everything in them, including God. When we are present, we join Dad in what He is doing and what He is up to in us and through us. We don't live in the past, future, or for the moment, but instead in it. It is good to understand that when we are absent we are operating from our false self, whereas when we are present we are operating from our true Self.

Let's face it. The reality is that all of us have a choice from where to live our lives. The Bible clearly tells us no wound, or demon, or principality, or power can separate us from the love of God. The choice is ours if we allow these to give us the false sense that we are separated from it. Instead, we need to always remember that we can only be as present with God as we are with the person or situation that is right in front of us.

What will it be for you today? Will you choose to live life from your heart where you will be able to trust Dad and enjoy the moment with Him, or will you choose to continue living from your mind where you will be led to be absent as you obsessively chase the same illusion of control that Adam wrongly purchased all those years ago in Eden?

PRAYER

God, I am wondering where I have been most of my life. One thing is for sure—living from this place called the now is what my heart desires. It is easy to see how this works when I see it from the heart. Yet I also know, only too well, how easy it is to get caught in it. Please help me to come into the reality of the now and understand that all I have is just that. You know, it is amazing how simple this spiritual journey with You can be if we are just willing to loosen our grip and focus on what You have placed before us. I too want to live like this, God, and to realize that the only way I will begin to see the helping hand You are always extending toward me is by staying present. Thank You, God, for this timely reminder and this truth I have never been able to see before. Amen.

POINT OF ACTION

Watch the sunset as many times as you can this week. Make sure you find a spot that is quiet and comfortable. Focus on the sun and the whole picture before you. Allow it to soak into you as you quiet your mind and focus only on what is happening right in front of you. As it comes to an end, write down the thoughts that attempted to break this moment up. Ask God what it is about these thoughts that is so important to you and why. Over the week, write down the differences that each day has had and how this exercise may be affecting you as you go about your daily routine.

NOTES

1.   Many of you who may have read *Holding On Loosely,* my first book, will know that my father is alive today because of the ability to stay present and not panic, despite him briefly dying in front of my eyes.

2.   This is clearly shown in the book of Ecclesiastes 3:4: *"A time to weep and a time to laugh"* (NASB). The way this works is that Dad would announce to them that they were now in a season in which to laugh. This meant that as far as they were concerned, they were going to laugh and laugh until the day they died unless Dad would say otherwise. Yes, I am sure they cried sometimes in this season too; however, the holistic picture was one of laughter. This only changed when Dad announced that it was now a time to weep, and so they would go on weeping until they died unless again Dad brought the season to an end. Living like this is impossible to do from our minds.

CHAPTER 9

THE MAN IN THE MIRROR

Submit therefore to God.
—James

I am going to start with the man in the mirror.
—Michael Jackson

G ood morning," I say to the tennis player I will be working with today. "Good morning, Pablo," he replies. I have been working with this young player now for a while. He comes from an affluent family where life is not too difficult, and the mentality is you get whatever you want when you want it. He is very talented but emotionally weak. Even though his game has improved, the way he lives makes it difficult for him to develop and grow. This immature approach to life leads him to become frustrated on the court when he is unable to do something I ask. My observations are mostly seen as a personal attack, and so tensions can be high from time to time.

This particular morning we have a blowup on court, and I end up sending him home before the practice is even over. "Dad,

I'm not sure what You were thinking when You made this one," I shout at the top of my lungs as I get into my car after leaving practice. "But as You are the One who made him, You can teach him to play tennis Yourself. I have had enough of this muppet and his baloney!" I am feeling frustrated and fed up with having to babysit him and deal with this every other day.

As I drive home, I begin to calm down, and James 4:7 rises up in my heart: "Submit therefore to God. Resist the devil and he will flee from you" (NASB). "What does that have to do with it?" I think. "Maybe Dad is trying to show me a way to get rid of this problem." After all this time, it is easy for me to believe that this player was being used by the devil himself to try and ruin my day.

Upon arriving home, I call a friend on the other side of the world, whom I speak to from time to time because he is also involved in tennis and understands my work better than most. During our conversation, I mention the verse I was given by Dad and share that I believe He is giving me the key to get out.

Upon hearing this, my friend laughs loudly. "It sounds to me more like He is showing you why this is happening, Pablo," my friend says. This remark stays with me for the rest of the conversation, even though we speak for another five to ten minutes about other issues. As I hang up the phone, I realize I have just been given insight. Perhaps, I am still asleep in some area that prevents me from seeing any direct truth as far as this situation is concerned.

"Dad, what am I missing from this?" I ask. "I know You are trying to show me something. But it is hard to see it when all I can think about is different ways to kill this player," I say, laughing by now.

"Pablo, you don't need to attach yourself to every word and action he says and does," Dad speaks.

"What do You mean?" I reply.

"You have a choice in how you respond to what he is saying and doing. You can either attach to it and get taken over by the negative feelings and situation, or you can choose to observe it."

"Observe it?" I ask. "What does that mean?" I walk outside onto my balcony for some fresh air.

"Well, when he becomes frustrated and cornered by a situation on the court, he feels the same feelings you are feeling. He feels the same frustration you feel, and he too wants to kill you. How about the next time this happens, instead of attaching yourself to these feelings, you simply observe them from within yourself." Dad continues, "When you choose to approach it this way, instead of reacting to what you are feeling, you can think of how you want someone to treat you if you were in the same situation, feeling what he is feeling."

"Okay, that's all great," I say. "But how will I be able to do this on my own or even remember it?"

"Submit yourself to Me within, and the enemy will flee," He replies.

With this last statement, I realize that what Dad is showing me is the difference between attaching ourselves to life by trying to fix and fight everything it can throw at us, or engaging with it from a place of peace and love. The reality is that as I engage from a place of peace and love, the change is remarkable in both the player and me. I no longer feel the need or the responsibility to fix or change him every time a potential argument looms in the horizon. I finally realize this was not my job, nor could I actually do it. My eyes were being opened to see the reaction that I was having was actually adding to the problem, not helping it.

To my surprise, the sessions became much more amicable. Over time, though, the change in him was not significant due to other reasons. I was nevertheless able to change and learn to empathize with him and others in their hour of need. This has not been a quick fix, but it is, in fact, an ongoing reality I am learning to come into as I am challenged daily.

The way we choose to treat others and label them is the same way we treat and label ourselves. Every time I judged (labeled) this player as immature and simply emotionally unstable, it was enough evidence to show me I didn't yet possess the ability to see beyond what hit the eyes of my flesh, and that I was immature and emotionally unstable. I now realize I was clearly seeing and approaching this situation through my false self and not from my heart where I am one with Dad.

This is what Dad was showing me through this Scripture: "Pablo, observe this from within where you and I are one and you are at peace." Like the sky observes the clouds going by, although it remains still and does not follow each one of them, we can feel the anger and feel the frustration, but we choose not to engage it. On our own, we will always attach ourselves to it, but if we practice seeing it from within, where God and we are one, we will enable ourselves to choose this other approach. This way, we will be able to do unto others what we would want them to do unto us, even when they don't appear to deserve it.

Some time back I was led to do something that was weird at the time—I was not sure what it all meant. As I look back now, however, I can see that it was Dad showing me the difference between a life that is always lived on the surface and reacts and is affected by everything that happens, and one that lives from the heart and is simply present and observant and engages when and how it is appropriate.

One summer morning I was at the beach and decided to take a swim in the ocean, which was not overly rough, but it wasn't calm either. I swam out enough to be able to dive to the bottom with my goggles on, then look up and observe the surface. While down at the bottom, I could see that the water above was choppy, yet at the bottom where I sat, it was still. This is a fantastic picture of what it looks like to observe life from within our hearts where we can choose how and if to engage the changing circumstances outside of us; or we can observe it from the surface of our lives, which is mainly our minds, where we are affected by the changing circumstances and feel the need to intervene and fix everything and everyone.

We need to honor what we feel and how we feel, but we do not have to be ruled by it. As we practice this, we will begin to find it much easier to avoid being ruled by the actions and words of others because we will be able to observe the offenses without taking them personally.

Jesus lived like this. He often felt anger and frustration, yet He submitted to the One within and observed the one without. Take, for example, where Jesus is being accused by the crowds while standing before Pilate. Many of us, unfortunately, miss this dimension at work through Christ on this occasion because we are far more aware of His divinity than His humanity.

We need to understand that Jesus was fully divine, but He was fully human too. This means He felt the same frustrations and ill feelings any human being would feel when accused of something that is not true. It was not that his response was available and possible for Him because He was more divine than the rest of us; His response was and is possible for any human, if we understand the concept of tapping in to the source we have within us—our God-nature and the presence of the Spirit. This enabled Jesus to observe the mess that was going on without having the need to defend Himself. He knew who He was and what the truth was. As He trusted and submitted to God within, He was able to see the reality that He who was within Him was greater than He who was in the world.

The truth is that Jesus felt all of this, yet He didn't attach to it. This is why He was still able to forgive the one thief and ignore the ridicule of the other, despite the personal suffering He was experiencing at the hands of His creation. We are called to love one another and do unto others what we would like them to do unto us, although, if we are honest, this is seldom done or experienced in the way Jesus meant. Jesus said is easy to love your sons and daughters and loved ones; it is easy to extend empathy to the one who has just blessed you with a new car or given you the break you have been hoping for over the years.

But can we do this to the man who just cut us off from the road and is laughing at us? Can we do this with the person who just slept with our wife, husband, boyfriend, or girlfriend? Can we do this with the tax collector who just sent us an unexpected bill? Or how about that person in church who makes that annoying and ridiculous noise we don't like every time the worship begins? The reality is that we will find all of these situations impossible unless we learn to practice self-observance.

"Pablo, you think you are always right," my friend says to me.

"No, I don't," I reply seriously—but I laugh now as I write this.

"Dad, if this is true, please show me as I don't believe he is right," I say on my way out of the meeting.

Days have gone by since this prayer, and now I am at the gym. During the workout, my trainer tells me that he saw me doing an exercise the wrong way the other day. As he says this, I feel a reflex-like reaction from within me that says, "No, I wasn't," which I then follow with a long explanation of why I was doing it right. While in the middle of the explanation, I feel something I have never felt before. I observe myself saying all of this outside from what I now know was my true Self within me. It is almost as if there are two of me: the one who is talking and blabbing away, fulfilling the urge and need to always be right, and the true me within wondering why I am saying all of this. No sooner do I come to this realization than I stop and say, much to my trainer's surprise, "You are right."

"Pablo, are you okay?" he asks.

"Yes, why?" I say.

"Well, you just spent three minutes trying to tell me I was wrong," my trainer says, "and then suddenly you said I am right."

"Oh, you mean that? Well, let's say I have just seen a side of me I never knew was there," I say with a smile. As we continue to work out, I know this puzzles him, although I am not puzzled by it. I have just been given a front-row seat to my life and the way I behave. I quite literally have just seen Pablo's false self's behavior from Dad's and other people's perspective.

This is what submitting ourselves to God looks like. The reality is that many of us cannot see because we seldom access life from our true Self. Most of our decisions and judgments are made from our mind and our false self. When we do this, we become experts in observing others and their behavior, but we never take the time to observe ours because we can't and don't know it is possible. We become self-absorbed instead of self-aware, which leads us to judge everything and everyone around us. One of the main ways many of us engage ourselves in this procedure is through gossiping about one another. Unfortunately, when we choose to do this, we are blinded to the fact that all our judging does is build the arena of our future failures, instead of leading us to the truth within.

We are born into a reality that is bankrupt, a reality that leads us to think and believe that we are bankrupt too. We ease this feeling by comparing ourselves to others. We compare the severity of our sins with those of others. We live with the mentality that yes, we sin, but at least it is not as bad as what that other person did down the road. We compare our accomplishments or the size of our companies. We compare the size of our churches, the reach our ministries have, or how important or well known the names of those with whom we associate. So instead of becoming students and observers of our own life, we take on the roll of ill-qualified judges who become well-seasoned professionals accurately describing and discovering the splinter in our brother's or sister's eye while failing to see the telephone pole in our own.

I want to share with you two stories I have experienced that have brought an amazing amount of freedom and healing to my life, but also to the lives of others. They will, I believe, help you understand further what this dimension of self-observance looks like when we practice it.

John first contacted me after reading my first book, *Holding On Loosely*. One conversation led to another, and eventually as I began to regularly share with him by email, I became aware that great shame was a close companion of his.

After several months went by, I found myself in Austin, Texas, speaking at a local church. Naturally, being in the same state meant I would contact my friend in Dallas. During one of our conversations, he mentioned there was going to be a small get-together at a friend's house in Dallas. He said it would be great if I could be there, although he understood it would not be possible. As I hung up the phone, Dad whispered into my heart, "Pablo, rent a car and drive to the meeting." I must admit I was tired from traveling, speaking at different venues; however, when Dad speaks, it is good to listen. I contacted John once again to let him know I would be coming. He and a few others kindly organized for my expenses to be covered, so to Dallas I went.

While there, we sat around a fire pit as I shared a few thoughts and experiences I had lived through. After this, we went around and everyone shared something about his own life. John's turn came up, and he began to share how he had been arrested for soliciting sex with a minor. He explained that he had done this by mistake, not knowing the girl's age at the time. He shared many more things, although when he shared the situation about the minor, I must admit I felt like a wall came between us. As I sat there, I chose to observe it from within and not give it any energy by engaging it with my mind. As he finished, I looked at him and gave him what I would have loved to have someone else do to me if I were in that situation.

I said to him, "I love you, and I think you are an amazing guy," which I quickly followed with a bear hug. I will never forget the tears in his eyes. But the amazing thing was that as he sat down, he said to us that it was really hard to share, and he felt ashamed as he began. I smiled because I realized the wall I had felt was the shame he was feeling. But because I remained present and observed it instead of judging it, I was able to empathize with him and do unto others as I would want them to do unto me.

Today, John is well on his way to recovery. Many have been the times he reminds me of this turning point in his life, especially when he heard that Dad asked me to drive six hours round-trip to be with him. John often says to me, "It still blows my mind that Dad thinks I am that special to Him that He would ask someone like you to drive all that way to be with me and affirm me the way you did."

The reality is that without the practice of self-observance in my own life, I would have never been able to see past the filters of John's offense. This would have meant not being able to extend the love and affirmation Dad knew he needed at the time. Only Dad knows where John might be today if that "I love you" and hug didn't happen around the fire that evening. One thing is for sure, it is highly unlikely that he would have anywhere near the healthy relationship he has with the lovely lady he is currently seeing, nor would he be starting to write his first book about his life and addictions.

The second story is a little bit closer to home as it pertains to my oldest daughter, Vanessa. During my divorce from her mom, she was the one who experienced the brunt of the situation. She was often, as many children are in this situation, the emotional punching bag in the family. My former approach to life that focused on perfect behavior meant she was trapped not only by her pain, but also by my false expectations and her attempts to fulfill them.

I will never forget when on one particular trip to South Africa, I realized she had become a chain smoker. Among other things, I felt angry and scared for her, and, at the same time, I also felt a deep disappointment by what I had just discovered. Here was my little girl harming herself through a habit that was probably being used to cope with much of the pain her mom and I had inflicted on her. I remember sitting alone on her couch with tears flowing down my face while feeling this, yet I chose to remain present and observe while I prayed. I knew that added to all she was feeling was probably a substantial dose of shame, as she worried about what I would think if I found out.

When she came home, I said, "Vanessa, I would like to sit down and smoke with you. I won't be able to smoke cigarettes, so I will smoke a cigar and, well, you will have to smoke two or three cigarettes until I finish because a cigar is far bigger than what you smoke."

"But, Dad, I don't—" she tries to reply, but I interrupt her.

"Come on, Nen," (as she is affectionately called). "I know you smoke, darling, and that's okay. I still love you and think you are great."

So we sat outside for hours talking, laughing, and just sharing life together while we smoked. Some months later, I found out that she had begun to give up smoking altogether, and I am happy to share with you that today, though she has the occasional cigarette, the habit is largely gone. The biggest breakthrough occurred when she told me, "Dad, the day you smoked with me, you gave me permission to embrace a part of myself I hated. The minute you did that, the desire to smoke and the shame associated with it began to disappear."

The truth is that the feelings I felt on the couch before she came home were the feelings she had because of her shame from smoking. Unlike other times with other matters, this meant I didn't judge her. Instead, I was able to love her in the middle of her mess, like Jesus loved me when I was in the middle of many of my messes. This ability to give her what I would have loved someone else to give me happened only because I was more aware of her and her cry for help than what I thought was right or wrong. I was able to prevent myself from giving in to the impulses of trying to fix, clean, and somehow rescue her from her situation.

All these superficial approaches would generate more degradation, because they only focused on trying to fix the symptoms instead of curing the root. It was clear to me by now that they were all based on gaining the right outward appearances instead of delivering inner healing and freedom into the person's heart. This will often take much longer, but unlike the other approach, this one will be real. It will lead people to a place where they will not just be healed, but they will also begin to live in a new reality where the change and healing they receive is not dependent on them continuing to work hard to keep it, because the change has begun within their heart. They have understood they are loved and accepted, no matter what they do or fail to do. It is important that we, therefore, understand that when we take the time to observe life, we come into the reality where we can literally witness the current of God's life and love flowing through humanity.

These were two separate incidents, two different people—but both with a similar outcome. We can do unto others as we want them to do unto us by being able to see them through the same eyes Dad sees them through—eyes that see through the behavior and focus on all that is lovely, pure, and true about them; eyes that understand it is far more important they hear and understand they are loved and embraced, even when they are standing in the most shameful and darkest parts of their lives, instead of blabbing away with all the quick fixes they need to suppress the symptoms they live under each day.

As I experience this truth and new dimension, the words of King Solomon in Proverbs 29:11 take on a completely different meaning: "A fool lets it all hang out; a sage quietly mulls it over."

I realize that what King Solomon was speaking about was self-observance. Paul also explained this approach and reality in First Corinthians 9:19-23:

> *Even though I am free of the demands and expectations of everyone, I have voluntarily become a servant to any and all in order to reach a wide range of people: religious, nonreligious, meticulous moralists, loose-living immoralists, the defeated, the demoralized—whoever. I didn't take on their way of life. I kept my bearings in Christ—but I entered their world and tried to experience things from their point of view. I've become just about every sort of servant there is in my attempts to lead those I meet into a God-saved life. I did all this because of the Message. I didn't just want to talk about it; I wanted to be in on it!*

Many of us often wonder why disciples like Paul had such wonderful experiences and saw the breakthroughs they did and we don't. I sincerely believe this happened because as they became fully aware of their pain and darkness, they were suddenly enabled to see and understand the pain and darkness in others. Paul told us he was the chief of sinners, able to do what he didn't want to and unable to do what he wanted to do.

If we are honest with ourselves, most of us do not live this way. We are mainly focused on protecting what we have, who we have become, and what we feel is clean, holy, and presentable. Our approach, unlike Paul's, leads us to a place where our lives become perfect soil for shame to thrive as we work harder, yet deep down we know that the lurking shadows within us are only getting bigger and harder to hold on to. People can see we are unable to relate with them as we have failed to relate with ourselves. Paul and the disciples understood that Dad felt at home with people who are real instead of well behaved.

The reality is that as long as you are not real with yourself and you don't face the reality of what life has led you to become, you will never be able to be real with anyone else, including God. We need to understand that when we approach life this way, we end up shaping our God and then that God shapes us. This is the reason a lot of people choose to stay out of church. They see within the church walls people who are out of touch with reality and how their life really is, and that their main interest is to fix and clean them instead of loving them the way Jesus did.

Let's face it. We love to put up this image of being winners and overcomers, yet we can't even be honest on a Sunday morning when we choose to smile although that is the last thing we want to do. We preach a gospel of power and guts, yet inside we are falling apart. People don't want to see Rambo in the pulpit on Sunday. They want to see Bambi—someone who is as weak and broken as they are, someone who is able to understand they are loved despite their weaknesses and shortcomings, someone who is slowly seeing a degree of healing in their lives, not because of how brilliant or strong they are but because they are beginning to understand how they are loved, as well as someone who understands that real maturity is not about being perfectly behaved as much as it is loving and having unconditional compassion for others all of the time.

I will never forget a man who came up to me after a men's event in a church where I spoke. "Pablo, can I speak with you?" he asks.

"Yes, of course," I reply.

"I am a Buddhist. However, I have been coming to these events over the years and listening to many people talk about Jesus because I am interested in His teachings. Yet I have never been interested or wanted to get to know the Jesus most of them shared because He struck me as being someone who was totally out of touch with reality. But, today, this Jesus you spoke about—I want to know Him. I want to find out more about Him," he says with a huge smile on his face.

The majority of us, like this Buddhist man, are desperate for a different kind of water. Like the woman by the well, we pretend to be someone we are not. We choose to invest our time and effort in comparing ourselves with others instead of discovering who we truly are. We need to understand it is impossible to see any degree of significant and permanent healing and change in our lives if we are not able to be present and observe ourselves.

If we are going to find this living water Jesus spoke about, then we need to stop looking for it outside like the woman by the well was doing. The water we can produce for ourselves outside is not designed to quench the thirst for intimacy we carry in our lives, and neither is it capable of healing us like the One we find within. The Bible is clear about this when it tells us that from within us rivers (not streams) of living water will flow out of our lives and into the lives of others.

The whole purpose of this journey is to reach that place within us where we enter into a reality where we are able to intimately taste and see that the Lord is good. Once here, we are set free to be able to suddenly love all and judge none because our journey is no longer about us as much as it is about others. From this place, we no longer find it necessary to wave our own flag in the name of being right or better in order to feel safe, but instead we are happy to let others wave their flags, and we still manage to love them and accept them like Dad does with us, no matter how wrong or flawed they might be.

PRAYER

God, it is not easy to ignore what others do to me. I have tried so hard to pretend that it didn't affect me, yet it did. I realize now that it is not about avoiding what I feel as much as it is about feeling it and owning it without being overtaken by it. Please help me understand that I can only do this from my heart and not from my mind, where I always feel I am on a mission to tell the world they are all wrong and I am right.

Thank You for helping me understand that this journey is not about who is right and wrong as much as it is about doing unto others as I would want them to do unto me. Please walk with me and help me see this happen in my own life, especially when I see those people You know I find so hard to accept and like. Amen.

POINT OF ACTION

Find a place where you can sit and where there are many people around, like in a shopping center. While being aware of your external experience, become concurrently aware of your inner state. What do you feel? What are you thinking about? What do you really see? How is the environment you are in affecting you? This internal awareness is the beginning of self-observation. You must intentionally turn a portion of your attention inward in order to observe yourself. It is essential not to judge or criticize what you observe in yourself. These emotions will distort what you observe and inhibit progress.

Once you have finished the exercise, write down the emotions you felt, how they affected you, and why. Please make sure you do this at the end, because doing it while the exercise is in progress will more than likely take you away from that place of contemplation and living in the present.

CHAPTER 10

OUR BIGGEST ALLIES

There is no room in love for fear. Well-formed love banishes fear.
—JOHN

Fear does not prevent death. It prevents life.
—NAGUIB MAHFOUZ

We failed, but in the good providence of God apparent failure often proves a blessing.
—ROBERT E. LEE

Within me there has always been an urge to focus on the next thing instead of enjoying what is right in front of me. The more I seemed to progress and accomplish, the greater the urge to look for more became. It was as if I were running away or, rather, I felt like I was trying to avoid something I feared. I will never forget the euphoria I experienced when my players won and the depression when they lost. Fair enough, no one likes to be defeated, although my reaction to it meant there was far more lurking within me than met the eye.

177

Over time, Dad revealed to me this persistent drive was actually powered by an unhealthy dose of the fear of failure. The way I saw it was that every time I succeeded, I feared more the possibility of failing and losing it all. As someone who was focused on getting it right and being accepted at all costs, success was the only suitable antidote to failure.

I remember one day walking into Wimbledon Centre Court and seeing the slogan: "If you can meet with Triumph and Disaster, and treat those two impostors just the same...." It was early in the morning, and few people were around, so I decided to stand there for a bit, taking in what I had just read. I quickly realized that Dad was trying to show me something through this quote. The word *disaster* stuck out. It accurately described how I saw and felt about failure. The reason failure was such a huge foe was because I saw it as the ultimate threat to the false image, the "me" I was so focused and dedicated to building and making bulletproof.

I will never forget Dad asking me as I began to walk away, "Your resume is looking good, but how about the condition of your heart?" Dad waited for me to find myself by the most famous court in the most famous tournament in the world of tennis to ask me this question. He could have done it in Australia, Paris, or even New York, yet He waited for me to be within the grounds of what many consider the pinnacle of tennis.

The reality was that my resume had labels added to it by the hundreds. My view that God only blessed those who got it right and were good added to this illusion I was chasing. Yet while all this was happening, every morning I woke up to a mixed salad of negative feelings, doubts, and fears that crowded my mind as they drove me to find new ways to somehow manipulate the future so I could continue this run of good results.

As I look back now, I realize how much I limited the reach of my life and relationship with Dad because I became a control freak. I avoided anything that was unfamiliar or that didn't fit into my small box of being 150 percent right and certain. Mystery observed me from a distance and faith was not even close to being a part of my reality. Today, I understand that in life we don't have results or outcomes; instead we have lessons and opportunities that are presented to us, although I, of course, didn't see this back then. I also realize that winning and losing is part of the way we box life to feel safe and in control. Unfortunately, our dualistic mind and the society we live in play a good support system to this way of seeing. There is nothing wrong with being successful and wanting to do well. But the problem occurs because we measure our worth according to success. The more we win, the more we believe God must be pleased with us; but the more we lose, the more God must be displeased with us. This schizophrenic way of gambling and bartering with life and God leads us to only one place, and that is to a complete spiritual and emotional burnout.

Those of you who have read my first book will know I ran out of steam inside a plane when I finally had to place the white flag over my head. I had come to the end of myself. In the eyes of the world, I was a successful man at the peak of his trade, but inside I was tired of running away from the fear of failure. The more I won, the more life was sucked out of me as bigger became the lot I had to protect and somehow keep. The thought of "I wonder when this good time will come to an end?" accompanied me most days. I realize now that I was never walking toward something as much as I was running away from something—failure.

The way I read the Bible meant I only focused on the big victories and the great breakthroughs. Great books like Job, Ecclesiastes, and even many of the red letters in the Gospels were avoided at all costs. I simply saw these as places where I didn't want to even look in case I heard or saw something I needed to change or give up. Inside that airplane I began to come to the end of my false self. I had by then given so much to it, and it had delivered nothing in return. Clearly, the event was monumental in many ways. I thought it was the end of me and all was about to be destroyed as I began to open my clenched fists and allow what I thought was my real life, although I now know it was my false one, to begin to slip away.

Inside that airplane, where I thought I was facing the end of my life, I was actually just getting started with it. We need to come to the end of ourselves if we are going to discover something new that has not been built up by our ego. Up until that point, my ego had been the king and main architect of my life. Yes, if you looked outside, it appeared that God had been kind to me, yet what was outside was delivered at the expense of what was in me, which was my heart and true identity.

Many of us have, unfortunately, been shown that all Dad cares about is our character. This sounds great on the surface; however, this is driven by a deep sense of shame and a fear of failure, not by grace and love. The approach of character development is measured by change of behavior and how well we are able to handle specific situations. Dad is suddenly seen as a hard taskmaster who doesn't care about our happiness and peace, but instead is obsessed with somehow preparing us for the promise of the heaven to come. Each time our lives are invaded by a lesson, we believe it has come to develop us further and make us purer and holier. Yet while we are hard at work with this mission, all along we miss the reality that everything we are working for is already within us.

This approach means we are prevented from seeing failure for what it really is. Thus, we miss what Dad tries to do through it. Our behavior and performance may improve for a time, but the amount of energy and focus it needs from us to keep it going means we have to forsake something else—our heart. Lessons are not meant to equip and change us as much as they are supposed to reveal something about us.

When we approach life through the eyes of our false self, we see failure as a result and a label that eventually can become our identity. We are given this false belief that the chosen ones don't fail, that failure is just another proof that we are still incomplete and flawed, and that our character still needs further refinement. I wonder what Paul would have thought of this approach when he took a look at the thorn in his side? Unfortunately, this is what most of us subscribe to, which then leads many of us to try even harder, although Jesus never called us to build a perfect identity outside as much as He encouraged us to discover the perfect one we had already been given within. Jesus was perfect and lived a perfect life, yet He was not a perfectionist. He knew that as we discovered our true Self, the behavior so many focus on would change automatically as a by-product of this discovery.

Most of us have totally missed the point of failure when we believe the gospel Christ brought to us is mainly about behavior modification and being part of a moralistic religion. What Dad is most interested in is in the condition of our heart. And failure is one of the best places where we can be shown what is really going on in us and the great impact it has on our behavior—if we remain still and don't try to run away.

Our misunderstanding of what Jesus came to say and show us also supports much of this false illusion. Many of us see Jesus as someone who was above us. Yes, we are happy to confess He was fully human, although we have a belief that He had something extra over us that led Him to be perfect inside and out. But do you believe that every coffee table Jesus built was perfectly straight? Do you honestly believe that even though He ran His bare hands over rough pieces of wood every day, He never got a splinter? Do you believe Jesus never tripped over one of the millions of rocks that were used to lay the paths in His day?

In fact, let's modernize these questions a bit. Do you believe that if Jesus were alive today, in the flesh, He would never take a wrong turn while driving His car? Do you think Jesus would never use the GPS to reach a location He had never been to before? If He played tennis with me, would He never miss a ball and just walk into Wimbledon and beat everyone there without a day's practice or hard work? The way we choose to answer these questions will give us a good indication to whether we truly understand the perfection Jesus spoke about and displayed in His life.

Let me be clear: Jesus never sinned. However, I do believe He made mistakes like we all make every day, because He was still 100 percent human. The Bible tells us this clearly in Hebrews 5:9: "And having been perfected..." (NKJV).

"Perfected" means that He also underwent a process of maturity and discovery. The aim of this process was not to get it right so as to gain a bulletproof character, but instead to discover His true identity. Like Jesus before us, our likeness with God needs to be discovered over time. This is why after Jesus is baptized He is taken to the desert where His real identity is questioned. Not His character, but His identity. I wonder why this didn't happen when Jesus was twenty. Perhaps He was not yet ready to face it as He was still undergoing the process of growing into the understanding of who He really was. If Jesus had access to something we don't, then the reality is that we are following someone who is not honest and true, and we are trying to reach a place that is out of our reach.

Jesus was perfect in His image and in His nature. However, like us, He had to undergo a journey of discovery. We have a misunderstanding of this because we equate failure and making mistakes with sin because we see it through our dualistic mind where there is either right or wrong. Clearly, in life there is a role and a place for dualism. Jesus used it when He said things like we can't serve money and God. Yet if we are ever going to be able to understand and see things like failure and fear as allies and friends, we need to see them through the wholeness of our heart and not with our dualistic mindset. Dualism may work to help us wake up; however, once awake, we can't continue to journey forward if we insist on seeing things as either black or white.

Failure is part of life—it happens often. It has happened to me and it has happened to you, much like it happened to Jesus. If we look at Jesus's life, we can be forgiven for thinking that it failed, yet it was through what seemed like a huge failure that the biggest victory was actually won. Jesus Himself had to walk through this experience, and even though He could have been bailed out quickly by legions of angels, He stayed present and went through with it because He understood that although He found Himself in a space of failure, He was not a failure.

> When we run away from the space of failure, we show that we are failing to see the bigger picture God sees in our lives, and it is the reason why we continue to usher ourselves into this space of failure over and over again.

I will never forget the day Dad showed me that failure was indeed the richest learning ground known to man. I was watching one of my players play a match in a big stadium full of people. She was supposed to easily win, but she complicated things for herself in ways that I could not understand. We had discussed the game plan, which was working well, until she decided to change it. As you can imagine, this ruffled my feathers as I sat on the sidelines unable to do much about it.

"Why is this bothering you so much, Pablo?" Dad asks.

"Well, because this is so stupid. She is going to lose a match she should be winning," I declare.

"But maybe if she loses, you and her will be able to finally see something you are not seeing when she wins," He replies.

"Well, it is obvious what is wrong," I say.

"Yes, but what is happening here is the reason why she loses easily to better players. She might be able to beat the lower-ranked players and just get by, but the minute the better ones show up, what happens?"

With this last remark, I realize what Dad is showing me is that I have totally missed the main reason why she can only beat the lower-ranked players but never the higher-ranked ones. I also see that my urge to build success and my false image has meant I never remained still long enough while this was happening to be able to observe what was really going on. All I could think about was how I could quickly fix it to gain the desired result, instead of discovering the healing and wisdom that was available as we walked through this space. The urgency that drove me led me to leave this threatening place quickly every time I found myself here. Every quick escape meant I would continue to come back to it. When we run away from the space of failure, we show that we are failing to see the bigger picture God sees in our lives, and it is the reason why we are being ushered into this space of failure over and over again.

She eventually lost this match, but for the first time I was happy because that day I had discovered something I never had been able to see before, even though it was right in front of me all along.

After the match, I went to my hotel room and got on Facebook. The first post on my news feed after I logged in was a quote from Michael Jordan:

> I've missed more than 9,000 shots in my career. I've lost almost 300 games. Twenty-six times I've been trusted to take the game-winning shot and missed. I've failed over and over and over again in my life. And that is why I succeed.[1]

This hit me square between my eyes. Failure is just a part of life. Dad is not upset or ashamed of us when we fail. Instead, He is happy to walk with us and help us discover, so we can move on in our journey instead of being stuck on the same lesson for the rest of our lives. We also need to understand that if we avoid this space called failure, we will have a hard time trying to discover who we really are. We might try to change careers, jobs, partners, coaches, and even hobbies. Yet failure, although it may look different in each of these places, will still be present in our path more regularly than it probably needs to be. This is because Dad is committed to helping us discover our true Self.

Someone who is awake knows how to fail. They are not scared of failing because they understand that when they do, they are actually growing because they are visiting a place they have not been before. Yet, as they remain here, they also know that they will eventually come to the end of this space. Seeing failure through the eyes of the love within our heart means that we understand the process and, therefore, realize that although we are experiencing failure, we are still moving forward instead of being on the side of the road, broken down and stuck. We realize that failure is not a result or our identity as much as it is a space we are traveling through. We need to remember that failure does not mean we have lost our momentum; it actually means we are in a space where we have the potential of adding to it if we take the time to observe and listen to what is going on around and within us.

> The reality is that we are not interested in people walking through this space of failure as much as we are in cleaning and fixing them. We do this in the name of discipleship and character development, but in my experience all that happens when we do this is that we prevent people from having their own discoveries and individual journeys.

We need to learn to be still and not agitated by our ego every time we are failing so we can have a better chance to discover what our heart is teaching us. This way, we make the most of the opportunities that are hidden within failure, which, if discovered, will lead us to have more of our heart available for the journey and fulfill the first commandment Jesus gave us—to love the Lord our God with all of our heart.

If we, however, choose to ignore it and focus ourselves on leaving this space quickly, we will actually regress and take a step backward and further into the place that holds us from discovering all life has and wants to show us. After reading the above quote by Michael Jordan, I read a story that showed me how Dad responds to us every time we enter a space of failure.

This story was about a young IBM manager. Once he finishes all his courses, his boss puts him in charge of a $25 million account. The young man accepts the challenge, so he goes to work. Three months go by, and he loses the account. So his boss asks him to come and meet with him to discuss what has happened. As the young man enters the boss's office, he immediately says, "Sir, I am very sorry about this mistake. I have failed you, and I am happy to accept my termination of employment." The boss stands to his feet and shouts, "Termination of employment—are you crazy? I just spent twenty-five million dollars training you!"

Do we believe this is how Dad responds to us when we fail? Unfortunately, we have not been consistent in responding with such grace, love, and open-mindedness as this boss at IBM did. In fact, too often we have seen how people are dealt with when they enter into a space of failure. This flawed approach is enough to show that it is a bad idea to find ourselves in a space of failure because we are indirectly taught through the treatment of others that it is better and wiser to keep whatever we are failing at within us and make sure it never comes out. After all, who wants to be embarrassed, ashamed, and feel like there is something majorly wrong with them?

The reality is that we are not interested in people walking through this space of failure as much as we are in cleaning and fixing them. We do this in the name of discipleship and character development, but in my experience all that happens when we do this is that we prevent people from having their own discoveries and individual journeys. The way of discovery is too risky and it will mean people taking longer to behave properly and do what is right, never mind not being able to control them. The discovery approach totally undermines the polished label and false image of Christianity we like to sell and present to the world, although Jesus never did.

If behavioral modification was so important, how come Peter's behavior didn't really change after spending 24/7 with Jesus Himself? If Jesus's main emphasis was behavioral change, then Peter would have been a very different man than the one we see when Jesus is arrested, yet he was pretty much the same man he was when he was invited to follow Him.

As long as we are not comfortable with failure, we will never be involved in anything more than the rat race everyone else is in. I don't know about you, but to me it is clear that only a rat can be involved in such a race. Because we are not rats, why are so many of us still taking part and conditioning others to stay in this race?

Jesus never punished or condemned anyone He met to hell, and He met His fair share of people traveling through the space of failure. I have to believe that unless Jesus dramatically changed His way of thinking and approach when He died and was taken up to heaven, then He still feels the same way about people who fail and make mistakes. We use hell as a weapon to scare people as the consequence of traveling for too long in this space of failure, yet what we fail to see is that what we focus people's attention on is what we empower over them.

In other words, if we make people feel uncomfortable and scared enough to leave this space of failure, what we are actually doing is empowering both hell and failure over them, as this is what they will spend their whole lives trying to avoid. Is this what we really want for ourselves and those we claim to love?

The Bible tells us that Dad is quick to love and slow to anger. The day we understand and learn to embrace the space of failure in our lives will be the day we are able to embrace other people and their spaces of failure—it will change our lives. This changed me when my approach shifted from being someone who used to say to his players they had to win no matter what, to telling them that it didn't matter if they won or lost as long as they played with all of their hearts. This discovery of failure led me to remind my players each time they traveled through this space that they were actually in the presence of answers and truth, because the word FAIL actually means Finding Answers In Life.

Ultimately, the main reason why most of us encourage ourselves and others to stay away from failure is because we don't understand who we really are or see things as they truly are. If we are honest, most of us are more interested in impressing others, our leaders, and even our families than we are in the condition of our heart.

Dad showed me something that revolutionized my view not only of failure but also of the fear of failure, which was the reason that, although I had accomplished much, I still felt like a failure. I had just finished my lunch on the plane and, after the flight attendant picked up my empty tray, I began to read my Bible. That day's verse was from John 12:42-43, which said:

> *On the other hand, a considerable number from the ranks of the leaders did believe. But because of the Pharisees, they didn't come out in the open with it.*

They were afraid of getting kicked out of the meeting place. When push came to shove they cared more for human approval than for God's glory.

"Pablo, when people don't know who they really are, they allow their view of failure to turn into a fear that rules and limits their lives," Dad whispers into my heart after I finish reading these verses. "In time, they are no longer able to take risks so they can grow, because the common denominator in their walks is fear and not faith."

As I sit there, I realize that when we have the wrong perspective on failure, we open our lives to a fear that is then responsible for driving us to deny our heart and what we really want, because we are too scared to pursue them in case we fail. The reality is that the only way we learn about failing is by actually failing. When we fail, it does not mean that we are suddenly out of control, and when we succeed, it does not mean we are not suddenly in control again. This concept is a lie manufactured by our dualistic thinking. The truth clearly shows that both failure and control are an illusion.

Do you enjoy your life the way it was meant to be enjoyed? How many times have you quit something that was designed to show you something new about you or, worse yet, you never even tried because you were too scared of getting it wrong? When we fear failure, we fear the road that is meant to help us discover who we really are. This fear that plagues us and that so many of us work so hard to somehow quiet does nothing more than show us there is something broken and wounded within us.

When we see fear through the eyes of peace and love along our journey, however, we understand it is nothing more than an alarm. When something within us that is broken and in need of healing is touched, what happens is that fear turns off because this is our natural response when we face something we know we can't handle. The problem is that we try to quiet the alarm by either quitting or running away from whatever has just touched us in this broken place.

This is the total opposite of what needs to happen. When an alarm goes off in our homes, we don't fix the alarm. What we do is undertake a deeper investigation, looking from room to room for the reason why the alarm is going off. When we find it, we change it and then the alarm automatically turns off—maybe a window was cracked or a door came ajar.

As I have begun to live out of my new heart, my view on fear and failure has been radically changed. I have come to understand that Dad's ultimate objective in each failure we go through is for us to discover our true identity, which will then enable us to live the life we are called to. In other words, if we neglect to travel through the space of failure, we will likely fail to discover who we truly are. It is that simple.

Too many of us miss the pearls of wisdom available in this space because we see it as a place where a preparation for something great happens, instead of a revelation where we are shown what is within us that is already great. Our fear of failure means we go into these places with the mindset of getting through them as quickly as possible so as not to feel or be in failure for too long. After all, we have great things to do for God, right?

The further down the road I travel, the more convinced I become that this whole journey is not about doing great things for God as much as it is about discovering our true identity and letting the great things be a by-product of undertaking that journey.

Unfortunately, our flawed perception of failure and fear will mean that most of us will never actually get there, because we will always be looking to stay away from one of the main places where this beautiful truth can be discovered.

The biggest transformations in my life have taken place while living in a space of failure. During these times, many of the boxes and vices I kept myself in to feel safe have disappeared as a new lease of life, freedom, and truth have appeared in their place. This book has been written because I have failed and discovered truth through my failings. The truth is that I still fail miserably each day. I say and do things I would prefer be different, yet I don't fight them off but instead submit myself to Dad and listen to what He has to say about the situation.

I also understand Dad travels through my failures with me. In fact, it is here where He wants me to know how much He loves me. Each time I fail, I am reminded again and again that on this journey of ours there is no sell-by date or deadline by which time we need to get it right. Some things, as we know from the thorn in Paul's side, will not be healed or changed on this side of glory. Does that mean that we give up or spend our whole lives trying to fix the problem? Absolutely not! We should know by now that results are Dad's responsibility. I believe the thorn in Paul's side and the ones we carry happen so that others can see that despite our shortcomings, if we have hope and know that we are loved, then there is still hope and love for them too.

I encourage you to take a risk and embrace failure and fear the next time they show up. While you travel through this space, be easy on yourself and patient—Dad is not in a hurry. He doesn't need to impress anyone, and neither do we. He is comfortable around failure, and we need to be too if we are going to be able to reach a place where we can express our true

Self and the life that is within us. Remember, you and I have never been nor will we ever be failures. If we were, then Dad never would have said that we are very good!

PRAYER

God, I feel such shame every time I get it wrong. If I am honest, I am so tired of the energy and effort I invest every day to try to shine through what I do. As I have read this chapter, I realize how scared I am of failing because I think this will ultimately be a reflection of who I really am. You know me well, and You know how I am so desperate to see others smile at me and tell me "well done" and how good I am. Yet I can see the only "well done" I need, I already have. Thank You that the same "well done" You spoke over Jesus is the same one You have spoken and will continue to speak over me for the remainder of my days. Please help me live from the reality where I am able to see that failure and control are empty illusions we chase as we try to build our false self. Thank You that You don't see me as a failure but as Your beloved son, even when I happen to fail. Amen.

POINT OF ACTION

Think of something you would like to do but are not very good at, and start doing it with this new approach I have just shared with you.

NOTE

1.   Nike, advertisement, 1997, accessed October 1, 2014, https://www.youtube.com/watch?v=GuXZFQKKF7A.

CHAPTER 11

IT WAS NEVER MEANT TO LAST!

*You are just a vapor that appears for a
little while and then vanishes away.*
—JAMES

Tradition is the illusion of permanence.
—WOODY ALLEN

Pablo, this is the last month you will be working with this player," I hear Dad whisper as I am getting ready to go to our first practice in almost four weeks. Hearing this puzzles me because I am supposed to be traveling with him at the beginning of next month for two big events in the USA. Still, I have just returned from another successful speaking tour around America, and I am still buzzing from all I have seen Dad do in so many lives. My attention is now fixed firmly on what is happening at the moment, and I am also excited about the future because I perceive what look like solid and permanent circumstances.

The end of the month approaches, and I'm supposed to be boarding a plane with him for America in just three days. I am excited because he is playing well and I feel he is finally ready to produce a noticeable breakthrough. We have worked extremely hard and have been through much together over the last year. There have been many ups and downs. He has continued to grow and is slowly learning the ropes of the career he has chosen to pursue. The final preparations and touch-ups are coming to an end. We are truly ready and excited as we look forward to the big events we will be traveling to in a few days.

"Come on, let's play one last set of table tennis," I say to my pupil as our second practice of the day comes to an end. This is not really table tennis, but a fun game we usually play on the tennis court in the service boxes where you have to make the ball bounce on your side before it goes over the net. It has become somewhat of an ongoing competition amongst the team to help them progress in their tennis career. We all enjoy playing it because it is a great warm-up and session finisher—not to mention the skills it develops—and it is a great excuse to have some fun in what can normally be a very intense environment.

Today, we have already played in the morning and I have won the first match. As usual, like we all do to one another in good fun, I have been reminding him at strategic times throughout the day over phone messages how I beat him this morning, which has naturally built up tensions so that neither of us can wait until the second set of the day takes place.

We begin our second set after practice is finished, and once again I manage to pull ahead in points. I am moving like a gazelle as I float and slide, like a true artist on the clay courts we are playing on this week. I am feeling great. As the game progresses, he makes a small recovery and suddenly the score reaches three to three.

After a few seconds of staring at each other while jumping up and down as two boxers do before a fight, I serve to begin the seventh and final point. We get into a heated exchange of shots as we both move and lunge ourselves all over the court. Suddenly, as I turn around and start to run for my next shot, I hear a very loud *pop*, and I fall flat on my face. I immediately look back to try to understand what this sound was and why I am suddenly wearing red clay from head to toe. I don't see anyone or anything, and I don't have any pain, so I stand up to replay the point. When I take my first step, I feel a shuddering pain travel from my heel toward my knee. It is almost as if someone has just stuck a knife in my ankle area. No sooner have I gotten up than I am falling back down to the ground.

I begin to scream and hold my leg, which is in some of the most excruciating physical pain I have ever felt in my life. By now, my player begins to realize that something major has just happened, so he jumps over the net and comes over to see if I am okay. "You have to get me in the car," I say, "and we have to go to see the physio. It is not good, mate."

Once we arrive, my physiotherapist examines me, then says, "Pablo, you have completely torn your Achilles tendon."

I ask, "What do you mean? How can that be possible?" I go to the gym every day, I have a regular body-strengthening program, and I run, cycle, and stretch at the end of each session. I eat well—most of the time—I don't really drink that much, and have the occasional cigar now and then. I have never had a major injury in all of my sporting life apart from the normal niggles one feels from pushing sometimes a bit too hard or the twisted ankle that recovers after a few days. I train hard, so injuries like this can be avoided. Yet, here I am, lying like a lifeless body on my physio's stretcher.

I am still trying to grasp what has just happened to me. Everyone is speaking Hebrew, which makes it hard to understand what is going on. My foot kills, my leg feels numb, and my heart is wondering what Dad's role is in all of this. Everything I have been working so hard to build is slipping out of my hands. I am in a foreign country, my wife is on her way but not here yet, and from what I am told, I am looking at a recovery period of six to eight months. I think about how I am supposed to be on a plane bound for America in two days, yet that trip is now clearly not going to happen.

"Pablo, I have spoken to the surgeon, and you are booked for surgery in two days," my physio says as he interrupts my moment of solitude and wondering.

"Okay," I say. "Is it that bad?"

"Yes, Pablo," he replies, "it feels like you have completely torn it where the muscle meets the tendon, which is the worst place. Normally, though, you can recover. It is unlikely it will be the same as it was before the tear."

I have had my fair share of moments like this one, where my life, relationships, or even my career have hung in the balance as sudden and unexpected news was delivered to me. My human impulse wants to scream, shout, and run away as I hear this latest report, yet from deep within me a peace rises up that helps me remain present in the situation.

"Pablo, the operation was a success," the nurses tell me when they wake me up after wheeling me into the recovery room. I have just undergone a two-hour operation to sew my leg back together again. I am half asleep from being under general anesthesia, so I can't understand very much. I turn my attention to the end of the bed where I see my lovely wife smiling at me. My eyes fill up with tears as I whisper to her, "I love you."

I turn my head to the other side and close my eyes. "This is too much to handle," I think. What only a few weeks ago seemed like a comfortable and exciting future shaping up had now turned into an unknown and mysterious future once again. Well, to be honest, it was anyone's guess where I would end up. Here I was lying in a foreign hospital bed with my left leg in a cast up to my knee while my player, with whom I had worked so hard, was on his way to the USA with a good friend. I was staring at six to eight long months of recovery in which I would have to learn to walk again. Oh, how low, dark, and scared I felt in that bed on that November morning.

Fortunately, I am released that same day from the hospital, and Madeleine, who has been by my side all this time, drives me home. I have been ordered by the surgeon not to move at all for three weeks. I am only allowed to go to the toilet, take a bath with some help, and move between the couch—where I spend all day— and the bed—where I spend all night. As the days go by, I slowly but surely begin to gain weight and lose my physical strength from not being able to do much. Most of the time, I'm stuck on the couch, hearing the traffic outside as life continues on. Yet, for me, it has come to what appears to be a complete standstill.

One particular morning, Madeleine has gone out to run some errands, so I am alone in the apartment. I close my eyes while listening to some music by the Irish artist Enya. I am fully present as tears begin to flow down my cheeks. I feel totally helpless and weak. My mind is still struggling to come to grips with what has just happened. "Dad, why is this going on? It was all going so well. I mean, we had a great time in America. So many people were touched. Emails testifying are still coming in. Work was going well. Why did this have to happen, again? I know You said this was my last month with this player, but was there no other way to get this done than to handicap me like this?" I try to scream but can manage to only blurt out a few words due to the weakness I am feeling, both emotionally and physically. I wait for a while, yet I hear nothing in return, which makes matters even worse.

Some days go by, and I begin to open my heart to hear what Dad wants me to discover through this new episode in my life. This particular morning, I wake up like any other day. I have breakfast and settle down on the couch. I look around the room and, before I have a chance to turn on the TV, I feel led to open my Bible and read Hebrews 11. I am not sure why until I reach verse 13:

> All these died in faith, without receiving the prom-
> ises, but having seen them and having welcomed them
> from a distance, and **having confessed that they
> were strangers and exiles on the earth** (Hebrews
> 11:13 NASB).

The last part of the verse jumps out at me. I ask, "So what does this mean, Dad?" As I lie there, I begin to think about my own experience in life. I think how I have found myself often, like I do today, a foreigner in a foreign land. I think about how this has become the norm and something I have inevitably become used to. I remember how in earlier days when this began to be my experience, I felt the distance of being so far away from my home. I remember how each time I experienced an amazing victory, or even a defeat in my career as a junior player, I never attached myself to the experience for too long because I knew it would be coming to an end. The time came to move on to the next place.

As I come to the end of my thoughts, I realize I am on to something here that will not only bring clarity to my current situation but a greater understanding about Dad and His Kingdom. I still remain puzzled as I think how different were the feelings I felt over the years, while I traveled since the day I left home at the age of 13, compared to the miserable ones I have when the things I have built or worked on so hard have come to an end.

As always, when I begin to discover something, I decide to take a look at Jesus and the way He approached His life. After searching the Scriptures, I stumble upon two passages in which I see evidence along the lines of what I am beginning to see. The first one I am captured by is the huge difference between Peter's immediate response in Matthew 17:4, when he first sees Elijah and Moses speaking with Jesus, and the response Jesus Himself has to this same event.

Instead of enjoying the moment and taking it in, Peter asks Jesus if he should build a tabernacle for each of them. As we all know, a tabernacle is a structure that, although it can be of light construction and moved, is nevertheless designed to hold something permanent within it, ranging from a place to worship to a place to live. It is meant to take something—an experience, a belief, a memory, or even someone's identity—and make it permanent. Jesus's response, on the other hand, is amazing and totally different. While Peter wants to build something permanent, Jesus wants to move along to the next thing.

This difference between their responses reveals not only why I had become so disappointed when my Achilles tore but also why I became so disappointed every time something that was good, prosperous, and permanent came to an end. I realize now I was beginning to discover that Dad, unlike me, is not into permanent things—not in the spiritual and certainly not in the natural world either, especially if what we build will limit us and our under-standing of who we are in Him and He in us.

My attention is now fixed on verse 9, where Jesus goes a step further by telling them, "Tell the vision to no one until the Son of Man has risen from the dead" (Matthew 17:9 NASB). Did He just tell them to say nothing about this great experience? I have to go back and read this verse again because I can't believe it. How can Jesus expect someone, especially Peter, to not say anything about what has just happened? If I had an experience like this, I would probably write a book or even start some sort of tribe in the place, just like many have done before me. Yet Jesus totally ignores Peter's suggestion to take this event and make anything permanent out of it. Instead, He tells the disciples to hold on to it loosely until He departs, because there is more for them to dis-cover between now and then.

Next, I continue by reading the passage where Jesus feeds the multitudes in John 6, where my attention is once again drawn to a couple of verses:

> The people realized that God was at work among them in what Jesus had just done. They said, "This is the Prophet for sure, God's Prophet right here in Galilee!" Jesus saw that in their enthusiasm, they were about to grab him and make him king, so he slipped off and went back up the mountain to be by himself (John 6:14-15).

Here again is a crowd who had just witnessed one of the most amazing miracles Jesus ever did—simple people who had noth-ing special to offer or proclaim about themselves. They are clearly touched that someone would do this for them. As they begin to recover like Peter did on the mount of transfiguration, they too respond to what has just happened by wanting to make something permanent out of it. Jesus senses this, but He again ignores their suggestion and withdraws from them.

Why is this Jesus's response every time something like this happens? Why is He not willing to let people build structures or even celebrate what He has done for them by doing something in return for Him that will last? As I lie there, I realize that Jesus knew that if He allowed them to make something permanent, in time these very experiences would be where they would end up putting their trust—not in Dad. He understood also that over time these structures would be used to limit Him and the way in which He could move. In other words, they would become boxes that would give them a false sense of security, feeling they somehow had it all figured out because they were part of something God had done.

Jesus further showed us that this was the case when He said, "But I tell you the truth, it is to your advantage that I go away; for if I do not go away, the Helper will not come to you; but if I go, I will send Him to you" (John 16:7 NASB). In other words, what He was communicating was that if He remained here with them, they would build a religion after His humanity and in the process miss a life lived in spirit and truth.

He further emphasized the dimension of impermanence and the need to hold on loosely when he told Mary in John 20:17, "Don't cling to Me," or encouraged us in Matthew 5:40, "If someone drags you into court and sues for the shirt off your back, giftwrap your best coat and make a present of it."

Much of my disappointment has come because I have been seeking to try to make things permanent. The wins and losses on the road, although they were important to me, were only building my false image. On the other hand, events like interrupting my career when I tore my Achilles tendon were affecting and revealing something much deeper than my futile attempts to find peace, happiness, and reality in permanent circumstances.

We all long to have a place where we can settle down and just build something that lasts, something that gives us the sense of control and security as it becomes routine and predictable. These desires are not wrong; however, it is how we become attached to them that makes a big difference. Please allow me to briefly explain how this works by showing you how desire works when we approach it in an unhealthy manner.

Out of nowhere a desire comes up, creating in you the feeling that somehow you are lacking something and you are not complete, which naturally leads you to want whatever it is you think you feel is going to complete you. To end this feeling of lack, you begin to struggle to fulfill this desire you are suddenly having. More often, at least at the beginning of our attempts, we fail, which inevitably leads us to experience unnecessary suffering, frustration, and sometimes, depending on why you have this desire, overwhelming depression.

The same happens when you are successful and manage to achieve and gain what you wanted. You begin to think of ways you can now protect what you feel has completed you. And rightly so—who wants to be incomplete? One of your main drives then becomes to try to control everything, as the fear of losing your newfound conquest is too much to bear or even accept.

If we are honest with ourselves, we will agree that every desire ultimately demands everything from us, including that which is eternal. The desire sells us this idea that what we obtain is going to last forever when, as we all know, there is no such thing, and this too falls under the grounds of impermanence.

It doesn't really matter what the desire is for. It can be anything from health, triumph, and riches to even us wanting to feel noble by wanting the well-being of someone else we like or love. We need to understand that the problem is not desire or even having those desires. Many within the Bible had them, including Jesus. This part of life is necessary, as without desires we will have very little driving us to want to discover new things, including God and the truth.

Where the problem rests is in the way we become attached to these sudden desires and the idea they give us of what will happen when they are fulfilled. We see it this way because we think we are incomplete and need to be complemented by something permanent outside of us.[1]

We need to understand that the true source of life, happiness, and peace will never be found if we approach our lives in this way. Now that I am aware of this false approach, I see why so much of my life has been spent trying to find happiness and peace through something I could build or be a part of, instead of what was already within me, which was just waiting to be discovered. Today, I see how foolish I was to think that I could find my happiness and my identity in something that gave the impression of being permanent, but could indeed be lost at any given moment. Every time things got interrupted, it was Dad allowing certain things to happen in order to show this to me. Unfortunately, due to my high performance view of life and Dad, I missed this truth because I thought what I was actually in was another trial to test my faith and to develop my character instead of revealing something new about my true Self and life as a whole.

"Nothing is permanent in My Kingdom, except Me and My word, Pablo," I hear Dad whisper.

"This makes so much sense," I think when I hear this. Now I can understand why people like Abraham and Moses, who never received the promise, were able to die in faith after seeing from a distance the promises they had been given. These guys understood we are all merely passing through this stage called life. They understood there was no use in attaching ourselves to a certain revelation or a sudden discovery. They understood that one of the biggest mistakes we can make is to try to box these in to something permanent, because this action carries within itself the danger of stalling our lives by preventing us from further discoveries and growth.

This truth, unfortunately, doesn't just affect us as individuals but, regrettably, it also affects those who are part of our lives. If we subscribe to this approach of finding our significance and identity in what we do and not in who we are, and we are in a position of leadership, whether it be a family, business, church, or any other institution, then it is likely we will end up using and sacrificing others to build something permanent for ourselves. Furthermore, this will also lead us to a place where we will be in danger of watering down and misusing the message we have been given to share with others—all done in the name of building something permanent.

The first time Dad tried to show this to me, I cut Him short. This particular day, I found myself in the customer service area of a large store. As I waited for my wife to be taken care of, I began to notice something. Here was a department within the store exclusively designed to keep customers happy, with the one aim to make sure they would return and spend their money here again. This was a good idea when it came to making money, because if they didn't take care of their customers then someone else would.

There was a particular lady I could see behind the counter say all the right things to an angry customer in the hopes of making him happy. As I sat there, for some reason at the same time I was witnessing this, I began to think about the church. I remember so well how I thought to myself, "Well, the church is not a business, so they are not in the business of having to keep people happy so they keep coming back." No sooner had I finished thinking this when I suddenly heard Dad ask, "Really, Pablo?"

> The moment we begin to make something permanent, the structure we establish has the potential to become the god we serve and keep happy.

I didn't ask for it, and neither was I focused on any subject at this moment in time that was even remotely close to what I have just seen and heard. Thankfully, Madeleine returned after Dad said this to me, so I attempted to distract myself with some shopping. The reality was that I had seen something I knew was difficult to grasp. Yet no matter how much shopping we did that day, I knew that although this conversation with Dad was over for now, it was clearly not the end of it.

Today, as I lie here on the couch, I begin to remember again the conversation at the customer service department. Suddenly, I pick up the conversation with Dad where we left off, much like two friends do on the phone after being unexpectedly cut off. It is as if I am invited to take a step back as one does to better appreciate the bigger picture. Dad invites me to take the revelation I had received from the department store and look at it from a different angle.

I think how I would feel if I were the leader of a community of people whom I had led to help me build a permanent structure that, let's say, cost me $10 million and still had an outstanding mortgage of $5 million. Would my sharing continue to be the same? Would I suddenly stop saying certain things I used to say freely before the building was built? Would I follow Dad's lead uninhibited, or would I consider where He is leading and how that would affect those who help me pay for the mortgage and the upkeep of the massive permanent structure? Would I preach a message I knew was true, but when heard could lose 75 percent of the congregation? Would I continue to follow Dad wherever He led me, or would I trade this for keeping people happy? Would I, in fact, build and promote His Kingdom, or would I focus on building a spiritual customer service department?

I know only too well how difficult it is when we depend on others to make it to the end of the month. Clearly, in a normal job situation, we are called to submit to others who are over us, even when they are not necessarily doing something the way we would choose to do it and according to what we believe. I also know that in a business situation, it is wise to keep customers satisfied in order to keep the business going because businesses demand that money be pumped into them if they are going to survive and grow. But can the same be said when it comes to spiritual matters and the spiritual development of people?

The moment we begin to make something permanent, the structure we establish has the potential to become the god we serve and keep happy. Furthermore, many of us compromise our message because we know the truth, even when it is said in love, has the potential to upset people and lead them to move on. This means less revenue and the whole operation being threatened.

I can hear some of you saying, "So, what you are saying, Pablo, is that it is wrong to have places of worship?" Not at all. The problem is not the places of worship or people getting together as much as it is the affect these can potentially have on us. If we are honest, these have an unusual ability to capture our mind and lead us to forget they are not our permanent homes, nor will we die if we are not able to be part of them.

Many people have been manipulated and told over the years that unless they congregate, they will fade away because Christians are like coals, meaning that together they glow and apart they fade. Fortunately, this is not true nor is it scriptural. If it were, then how could men like Moses, Enoch, and Elijah, to name but a few—who had no Bible to read or a place to congregate—walk with God? This need to find something permanent to which we can attach ourselves comes from our misinterpreted need to look for our permanent home through our false self. This becomes apparent when we finally begin to live our lives from our true Self.

In James 4:14, the Bible says, "You don't know the first thing about tomorrow. You're nothing but a wisp of fog, catching a brief bit of sun before disappearing." And in Psalm 103:15-16, it says, "As for man, his days are like grass, as a flower of the field, so he flourishes. When the wind has passed over it, it is no more, and its place acknowledges it no longer" (NASB).

If these two verses are true, and our lives are indeed like a vapor or the grass and flowers of the fields, one minute here and gone the next, then why do we seek to make so much of our lives permanent? The reality that Jesus understood and that we need to understand too is that it was His life and not the permanent structures He or others built in His name that would go on making an impact in other people's lives. It was the way He loved and we love others that would make a permanent difference in our lives, because this is what we are all after at the end of the day. He also understood that permanent structures had an unusual way of dividing people, as they were led to think that life is divided between those who are part of the structure and those who aren't. Labels are also prone to thrive as we begin to build a culture around the permanent structure that loses touch with reality as it removes those who are part of it from the very society they have been placed in. As all of this happens, we also fail to understand that the family of God is made up of every single individual in this world and not just those who attend or are part of the permanent structure.

Have you ever wondered what our real aim is when we build structures, movements, theologies, and belief systems? I know as a coach that if I do my job properly, then I will work myself out of a job as I help my players understand what it looks like to be able to function without me. Do we do this with those whom we share life with through the permanent structures we build? Clearly, I don't believe any of us want to limit anyone else; however, do we encourage those around us to launch on to their own journeys and discoveries? Furthermore, is our teaching based on aiding an individual journey of discovery or one based on corporate dependence and the fulfillment of the vision?

If our intention is not to invite people into an uninhibited journey where they can discover the truth that is already within them, then what we are really doing is inviting them to a place where their emotions will need to be buffered on a regular basis to keep them happy. People need to be taught that the food for their lives is delivered by Dad anywhere and at any time, not just within a permanent structure on Sunday morning. We need to understand that meeting corporately was never meant to be central to our walk as much as it was meant to be complementary.

As I have looked back in my own life, I see that there are some symptoms that show up consistently in our journey when the main objective is to build something permanent for ourselves. As you consider your own path, it may be easier to understand if this silent killer of potential is present in your motives like it has been so often in my own life. The symptoms are:

1. Always having a need to explain instead of express yourself (Luke 20:2-4).

2. Always looking for an end result in everything you do (John 3:1-12).

3. If someone disagrees with you, you feel the need to try to convince them, and if they don't listen, then you look to others to give you the nod that the other person didn't (John 12:42-43).

4. Becoming instead of being (Matthew 16:24-26).

5. Purpose driven instead of identity led (Matthew 5:48; Proverbs 4:23).

6. Absent living (Matthew 6:30-33).

7. You seek to always make things permanent instead of temporary (Matthew 17:1-9).

8. You are more interested in how things are done instead of understanding why they are done.

As time comes to an end, I realize the importance in my own life of holding on loosely to my jobs, discoveries, defeats, and triumphs. I see now why Jesus said to follow Him, not camp around Him. Like Him, we also need to realize that our real and permanent home is within us where we are eternal, yet not permanently stuck. The impermanence of our bodies reminds us of this reality. Although we live within time, our lives are about connecting with that part of us that is not within time and that goes on living even when time is up. Here in this place we find the purpose of our life and the fellowship that sustains us, whether we are able to meet with others or not.

If you decide to build a permanent structure of any kind, please make sure it is not a limiting burden on people. Instead, aim for it to be like a liberating Ebenezer who reminds those around you and future generations of what happens when people are encouraged to discover the timeless reality that leads them to live from that mysterious, eternal, and true Kingdom that has been within them all along.

PRAYER

God, I must admit this walk to enlightenment is definitely not an easy one. Please help me understand that enlightenment can be a destructive process, and that it has nothing to do with becoming better or being happier as much as it is the crumbling away of untruth. Father, I don't want to see life anymore through the facade of false pretense. I want to see this life through the eyes of truth, and I can now see that this truth is not something we can bottle up and control.

Please help me understand this every time I try to make the discovery of a new belief or experience permanent within my life. I want to find my security and support in You and not in what I can do or the institutions I belong to. You are the source of my life. Thank You, God, for everything I am being shown. Please help me not get distracted by trying to master it all in one go, because this is a journey, You are not in a hurry, and, therefore, neither should I be. Amen.

POINT OF ACTION

Take some time in the next few days to ask God to show you what some of the things are you have worked so hard to build in your life to provide you with that feeling of permanence. Once you have clarity on at least one thing, take some time to reflect on how the approach you have been taking might change or look like now that you are aware of the false security you have been looking for. Write down how this former approach might have limited what you have been building. What new ways would you pursue now that the motives for building have changed? Put together a simple action plan that will help you implement some new steps to make this shift a reality.

NOTE

1.   Inspired by a post by Jim Palmer.

CHAPTER 12

INTIMATE PRAYER

With a God like this loving you,
you can pray very simply.
—Jesus

In prayer, it is better to have a heart without
words than words without a heart.
—Gandhi

It is a beautiful morning in Tel Aviv. The sun is shining bright and the temperature is perfect once again. There is a great feeling of warmth around, yet there is also a gentle breeze that is keeping my body cool. I am on my way to a work meeting where some business issues need to be discussed.

The man I am meeting with, an Israeli by birth, has spent much time over the years in India where he runs workshops on intimate prayer. He is Jewish by birth but classifies himself as a Buddhist and is, in fact, a Zen master. In years past, I would have attended a meeting of this nature by holding my cards very close to my chest. My religious radar would have been on a maximum state of alert as I watched for any possible demonic or dark spiritual agents trying to infiltrate my life through him. In fact, I would have probably discounted this man way before the meeting ever took place along with every word he spoke, because my belief was that nothing good could possibly come from a person who claimed to be a Buddhist.

Today, however, is a different story. I am grateful to say that Dad has dealt with much of my spiritual arrogance and sense of elitism that led me to believe that because I thought I owned the truth, I also had the right to decide through whom and when God's truth would be shared with me. I try not to think of the many opportunities I must have passed by in my journey in which I could have discovered so much more than I did. The times are too many to count as I look back now where I can see Dad's fingerprints all over someone or something that was meant for my good, yet I missed it—like the Pharisees missed Jesus—because it didn't come packaged the way I thought it needed to be.

"Shalom, Pablo, mashlomja," my friend says in Hebrew as he greets me.

I reply in my limited Hebrew, but I am genuinely pleased to see this man today after such a long time. I smile and make sure he knows this through my embrace. We sit down and spend a few minutes catching up on life and what has happened since we last spoke. He shares that he has been to India to run several workshops. I listen with interest and respect, following every word he speaks. I also share with him where I am in my journey with Dad and the things I have been discovering. It is a beautiful moment.

The conversation develops into work matters until we reach the point where we begin to speak about prayer and meditation. "Pablo, the problem with you Christians is that you don't understand prayer at all," he says with a smile, then taking a sip of his coffee.

"What do you mean?" I ask.

"Well, I have seen how you guys approach prayer on the Christian TV channels," he says.

I know exactly where he is going with this. But I play along and inquire further by asking, "I don't understand. Can you explain what you mean?"

"Well, when you guys pray, it is the same as when someone goes shopping. You come to the higher power with a shopping list of everything you need and want. You talk all the time, and when you have finished covering every topic on your list, you say amen and walk away. Then you invent formulas to somehow get the higher power to give you what you want. If they work once or twice, you write a book and sell it," he explains. I smile and say nothing for a moment.

"You are presuming all Christians are the same as the ones on the TV," I say, realizing, unfortunately, that from my experience most of us truly are this way. We have quiet times, yet we are anything but quiet. We attend prayer meetings and spend 98 percent of the time talking to God, yet only 2 percent listening to Him. Our needs are so often more important than He is, and, generally, we are more aware of what we want from Him than what He wants from us.

"Well, I see prayer completely different than this," he says.

"Oh, really? Do you mind sharing it with me?" I ask.

"Well, for me, prayer is a moment of intimacy where much happens and very little is said. Just like when two people make love. There is no way I could ever pray from my mind the way those people do on TV. That is not prayer. That is like a student reading an essay to their teacher. To me, prayer has to flow from the heart and not the mind. I need to connect with that part within me where I find my godlikeness," he says.

As my friend speaks, I realize that Dad is showing me something important. My heart knows that I am being given insight into an area I have often struggled with over the years. I have worked myself through just about every formula and "how to" manual on how to pray effectively, yet more often than not, I end up hitting a brick wall because my experience clearly does not match or even come close to the experience of intimacy my friend is sharing with me.

"This is the place where intimacy comes from—not our mind," he says pointing to the center of his being. "You see, there are three ways one can approach intimacy. The first is to get like those guys on TV I mentioned earlier. The second is to give in order to get. And the third is the way I approach it and that I believe is the only real way, which is to lose ourselves in the moment. We simply go in there with no conditions, expectations, or demands. We allow ourselves to be taken wherever our lover wants to go with us," he explains.

"In fact, Pablo, if you want to really know how you respond to an intimate spiritual moment," he says, "take a close look at how you respond when you are having an intimate moment the next time with your wife."

"You know," I say, "so much of what you have been sharing reminds me of a quote from Mother Teresa when she says that we need to find God, and He cannot be found in noise and restlessness. God is the friend of silence. See how nature—trees, flowers, grass—grow in silence; see the stars, the moon and the sun, how they move in silence. We need silence to be able to touch souls."[1]

Eventually, our morning meeting comes to an end. Before I stand up to leave, I look my friend straight into his eyes and thank him for sharing with me. I promise him to look into this further because I believe there is much truth in what he has just shared with me. We embrace once again, and I tell him that I love him and proceed to walk away into the distance.

I'm curious what Jesus had to say about the subject my friend and I were discussing. My attention is turned to Matthew 6:5-13 where Jesus speaks quite bluntly about what is accurately described as intimate prayer. I love how He goes about describing what prayer isn't and then finishes the passage with the most simple yet complete prayer anyone has ever come up with.

> *And when you come before God, don't turn that into a theatrical production either. All these people making a regular show out of their prayers, hoping for stardom! Do you think God sits in a box seat?*
>
> *Here's what I want you to do: Find a quiet, secluded place so you won't be tempted to role-play before God. Just be there as simply and honestly as you can manage. The focus will shift from you to God, and you will begin to sense his grace.*
>
> *The world is full of so-called prayer warriors who are prayer-ignorant. They're full of formulas and programs and advice, peddling techniques for getting what you want from God. Don't fall for that nonsense. This is your Father you are dealing with, and he knows better than you what you need. With a God like this loving you, you can pray very simply. Like this:*

Our Father in heaven,
Reveal who you are.
Set the world right;
Do what's best—
as above, so below.
Keep us alive with three square meals.
Keep us forgiven with you and forgiving others.
Keep us safe from ourselves and the Devil.
You're in charge!
You can do anything you want!
You're ablaze in beauty!
Yes. Yes. Yes.

I read the passage again and again. I can't help but see that so much of what my Buddhist friend shared with me this morning is right here in front of me. Starting with verse 5, I remember my friend's description of the people he saw praying on TV. Then, as I read verse 6, I once again remember what he shared about how we can approach an intimate moment. Verse 7 reminds me of the shopping list he spoke about and the approach of coming to Dad in order to get. Then as I read the prayer Jesus shared with us from verses 9-13, I can't help but think that if this is how He encouraged us to pray, and the prayer is that short, then what exactly did He do up on the mountain all night while He prayed?

As I ponder all of this—especially the phrase, "With a God like this loving you, you can pray very simply"—I realize this prayer was to cover just about every single angle of what we would need while on earth. However, what about the rest of the time? What do we do in our quiet times?

As soon as I have asked this question, I have a picture of myself holding my kids in my arms. I think how much I enjoy it when they sit with me, allowing me to feel their presence and touch. I don't want them to say or do anything. I just want them to let me love and enjoy them—no need to talk, no need to do or try anything, but be still. They are relaxed enough to go with me wherever I want. They have no control and are happy with this feeling of submission. This picture describes what intimate prayer is meant to look like.

"That's what I long for too, Pablo," I hear Dad whisper. By now I am welling up as I think of how many times I have gone into a prayer time with my shopping lists, formulas, and peddling techniques instead of with the willingness to just lose myself and see where He takes me—always more concerned about what I needed to get, even thinking about it while I mumbled words out of my mouth in what I called praying.

"Forgive me, Dad," I mumble as I sit there still and quiet. I spend some time here in this place enveloped by Dad's warmth and presence before moving on.

Some days go by, and I find myself in Pennsylvania where I have been invited to share with the men's group of a large church. A close friend of mine has organized for my family and I to stay in a small resort that boasts one of the most famous playhouses in America. I awake very early the first morning there because I am still somewhat jet-lagged from the journey across the Atlantic. My wife and daughter are asleep, so I decide to go outside to spend some time on my own.

As I walk out, I am met by a wonderful fall day. The skies are blue and the sun is beginning to shine. The trees have already started shedding their leaves, so there is a vast and beautiful array of colors all around me. The air is fresh and the noticeable feeling that every change of season brings with it is certainly here too.

As I venture out, I decide to go to the end of the property where there is a large stream. There is an unbelievable silence around me, and it doesn't take me long before I realize that the view and ambience I find myself in has already begun to penetrate my heart without permission. When I arrive at the water, I feel a strange invitation by Dad to go into the middle of it. It is very shallow, so I decide to follow. As I take each step into the water with my bare feet, I sense an amazing presence I have not felt before.

"Dad, I am ready to lose myself in You this morning," I whisper. I close my eyes and open my arms as one does when seeing a long-lost relative after many years. I feel Dad dancing with me and around me. My heart is alive, and my mind is completely still. If I have ever been more present than in this moment before, then, well, I must have missed it. If anyone would see me now, they would wonder what was going on. Yet as far as I am concerned, I probably feel the same way Moses did when he stood before the burning bush. I can feel myself being taken along, when without warning, I sense myself closing up just at the very moment I am beginning to feel Dad take me deeper. I don't understand why, but this is my reaction. I don't question it, but just accept it as I recognize this is a similar feeling I have within when I find myself in a very intimate moment with my wife.

"Trust Me, I am not going to hurt you," I sense Dad telling me. I know my reaction comes from the pain I experienced as a child and the many times people used and abused my vulnerability and generosity. I begin to cry as I feel something loosening within me. Tears are flowing down my cheeks as an ache within my heart surfaces and works its way out of my being. My arms begin to open up again as I no longer feel the need to guard myself. I realize that within that ache, there was also shame and embarrassment of what my reaction would be if I decided to lose myself in the occasion.

I spend many amazing and life-changing moments in this stream of water in the middle of Pennsylvania. Although there is a chill in the air, I still feel amazing warmth around me and in me. I am so grateful and feel humbled. "Thank You, Dad," I say. "Thank You that this is what You long for and not a captain/soldier relationship. Thank You for helping me stay open so I can listen to Your voice through my friend back in Israel. Thank You. Thank You. Thank You." My heart is overflowing, like David's cup does in the Psalms, and the way I would imagine he felt when he danced before the Lord.

I try to imagine what that day must have looked like when many missed the intimacy in this scene. Although it transpired in public, the whole event was nothing more than a very personal moment between David and his God. Others got to see it, but they didn't understand; hence, the label and shame they tried to attach to it. I understand why people needed to do this—it would have been the natural reaction of most who saw a king dancing in his underwear before the Lord. Yet for David, it was all about letting himself go and letting Dad take him wherever He wanted. This day, the luring took the form of dancing and letting it all hang out in the streets. While those watching saw the spectacle outside, I believe Dad and David were not aware of the external show as much as they were aware of the intimate moment they were both sharing while they danced.

I remain in this place for a while longer before exiting the water and working my way back to the resort. As I walk back, I feel so light and free. I wish I could describe it all, but the fact is that words fall short of what I have just seen, heard, felt, and lived. Suffice it to say, my prayer life will never be the same after this day and neither will be the way in which I approach intimacy in my life. The door of my understanding has been flung wide open to be able to start seeing what real prayer and intimacy are all about.

I understand that those who choose to avoid intimacy are normally people who do not know who they really are at any significant depth—neither can they tell others who they really are. It is from this place of softness that God is able to show us who He really is. Those of us who avoid this intimate way and prefer the self-sufficient and self-righteous approach will remain outsiders to the mysteries of divine intimacy and love. By choosing this way, we block ourselves from all the possibilities that are available to us because of the hardness we choose to maintain and carry within our hearts.

I no longer see prayer as a chore or something that has to happen at a specific time every day. Although, if it does, that's okay too. The words of Paul in First Thessalonians 5:17 (NASB)—"pray without ceasing"—which I struggled with for so long, began to make more sense. Paul never meant for us to be on our knees all day long, but he encouraged us to be aware of and in direct relationship with Dad throughout the day as we remained present and lived in the moment with Him. This is what intimate prayer is—after all has been said and done, we are intimately present with Dad each moment of every day. It doesn't matter if this takes the form of silence, talking, listening, or just simply being. What matters is that we are aware of His presence and love for us at all times.

In all honesty, I can't give you a formula or a specific spiritual description of what happened that day in the stream in Pennsylvania. All I can say is that from that day on, I entered into a new place in my spiritual journey and relationship with Dad. The days of trying hard to pray and spending hours on my knees trying to convince God to do something have slowly departed. In their place, a peace has surfaced that has surpassed all understanding. (See Philippians 4:7.)

Instead, into my life have come the moments when, without saying or doing anything, I feel and sense Dad's presence within my heart. In fact, it is surprising because even as I write this, surrounded by hundreds of students in the library of Tel Aviv University, I sense His sweet presence and love for me. This is the kind of intimate prayer I believe Jesus enjoyed up in the Galilean mountains when He continued in prayer all night. I believe something that transcends every word we can speak took place as He lost Himself in the moment with His Dad—just Him and Dad—no formulas, no recipes, no manipulative techniques—just His Father and Him spending intimate time together.

There is clearly a time and place for a quick prayer and a cry for help, which I know Dad also answers just like He also wants us to ask Him for what we need. The thing I am discovering is the more time we spend inside the practice of intimate prayer, the easier it is to have faith that these quick arrow prayers, like the ones Nehemiah or even Jesus prayed, will be answered. I know I thought I was attempting to have this kind of relationship before with Dad; but I now see it was futile as I was trying to do it from my mind and not my heart. Probably about 90 percent of all those times in the past I was more interested in seeing my shopping list met than I was in enjoying Dad.

While on one of my very first visits to Tel Aviv, I was just starting to work with a player from Israel, and, in between tournaments, we had a few days off while she fulfilled some sponsorship duties. Because I was staying by the beach, I decided to venture down and spend the day soaking up the sun and swimming in the beautiful waters of the Mediterranean Sea. At the time, I was reading a book called *The Shack* that had on the cover a small but distinct ladybug that played a major part in the storyline of the book. I lay there on the sand, putting the book down and telling Dad how much I longed to have an experience like Mac, a character in the book, had with Him in the middle of the forest.

I told Dad, "It would be great to have a simple sign from You to know that You are up for such an encounter with me." No sooner had I finished saying this than my over-reactive and performance-orientated mind took over as I put the book down and began to think of the things I could do to improve the player's game instead of just continuing to enjoy the moment. I spent time thinking about this while feeling a tickling sensation on my back. I didn't bother to check what it was because I was too busy working out ways that would help me manipulate my future.

Eventually, I gathered up my belongings and began to get up from where I had spent much of the afternoon. Strangely, as I did this, I began to feel the same tickling sensation on my back once again. This time, however, I reached around to finally see what was causing it. As I brought my arm back around, I will never forget seeing a bright red ladybug walking on the palm of my hand.

The only ladybug I have seen in Israel since that day had an orange-colored shell, not the bright red one this one had. I know

Dad put that on my back when I asked for a sign, because it looked exactly like the one on the cover of *The Shack*. This was Dad's way of saying, "Yes, I long for the same encounter too, Pablo." Yet, I realize what a muppet I was to miss such a close and personal touch from Him, and all because I was too busy and absent thinking of how I could make the future I needed happen. If I had only remained in that intimate moment a while longer, I am sure my life would have been enriched far more than any manipulative formula I might have come up with that day on the beach.

With everyone I see, I somehow sense His presence as I become aware of Dad's playful nature at work before my very eyes. More than ever before, I realize how closed and wrong I was when I thought that Dad could and would only want to show up when I prayed at my set times. I think about how I missed Him in nature and in all He has made.

As I have continued to practice this kind of intimacy with Dad, I see so much of Him and His fingerprints in just about everything I look at or that crosses my path. I seek to live my life in a road established and kept by grace, from which I am able to notice the romance that Dad has going on with everything He has made. More than ever, I can also understand why He was not in the earthquake, the fire, or the gushing wind, but instead inside the still small voice when He spoke to Elijah outside his cave on Mount Carmel.

I am coming to a place in my journey where I understand that if I want to hear Dad speak aloud, all I need to do is take a look at the huge waves of the ocean in front of my apartment, or the roaring rapids in a river, or perhaps hear Him in a nice electrical storm, or even in the thunder that ushers it in. If I, however, want to hear Him intimately speak to me, then I need to allow Him to take me wherever He wants as I lose myself in Him—not with my mind, but with my heart.

While watching a National Geographic program, I was given a picture that described what being still and fully surrendered looks like. Here was a man in the middle of the jungle wanting to see and film a rare and exotic animal that very few had ever seen. He tried and tried, yet he didn't seem to be able to capture it with the lens of his camera. He decided to approach a local person to ask him what he needed to do. The local man told him that if he wanted to see the rare and exotic animal, then he had to be quiet and still a lot longer than he had been up until then. He said, "They come out when *they* are ready, silent, and how they want, not when and how you want them to."

How often are we still and quiet, and for how long, when we pray? When was the last time we prayed and said and thought about nothing for more than one or two minutes? When was the last time we felt Dad's touch when we were in the middle of doing something? When was the last time we took time to go out into nature and share the moment with the One who made it all and in whom all is found? The reason why it is good for us to be still when we pray might not be to give Dad time to show up, as much as it is about us detaching ourselves enough from the restlessness that prevents us from seeing that He is already there.

We can all learn to go deeper and understand something new. None of us has it all figured out. This chapter would have never been written if I had approached that meeting in Tel Aviv with the same elitist attitude I once had. I meet so many people who tell me God never speaks to them and they can't hear or see Him in anything, let alone everything. Strangely, these are also usually the same people who struggle to tell me who they really are. It is impossible to understand who we are and how Dad feels about us if we never take the time to listen and see.

There is a big difference between rhetorical and intimate prayer. One is a chore and the other is a lifestyle; one is centered within our false self and the other in union with Dad; one makes us blind and deaf, while the other opens our eyes and ears so we can see and hear; one leads us to a dead end, while the other to a spacious place where we discover who we really are; one keeps us outside of ourselves, while the other helps us navigate inwardly into our true Self; and one happens at set times of the day, while the other with every passing moment. I know which one I desire for my life. Which one do you desire?

PRAYER AND POINT OF ACTION

I want to encourage you to use this time of prayer as an opportunity to practice what you have just read. If you are up for it, I want to invite you to settle down somewhere you know you won't be disturbed. Close your eyes and place one of your hands on the middle of your being, just below your chest. There is no need to say or do anything. Just sit there for a while and allow your being to be centered. As this is happening, whisper, "You are here. I am here. We are here together." Keep sitting there and take in what you have just whispered. If you have time and feel you want to continue, then do so by whispering, "Who are You? Who am I? Who are we together?" Continue to sit and enjoy the moment as you and the lover within enjoy one another, intimately connecting heart to heart. Please don't worry if you are unable to reach this second whisper. You can always do it the next time you pray because, after all, there is no rush in this journey of ours.

NOTES

1.   I am paraphrasing this quote I read from Mother Teresa.

CHAPTER 13

ONE

That they may all be one; even as You, Father, are
in Me and I in You, that they also may be in Us.
—Jesus

Each one of them is Jesus in disguise.
—Mother Teresa

I am only too aware that this probably is the most misunderstood and misinterpreted subject about wholeness that includes our heart, true identity, and who we really are. Many of the struggles and fights I have been through had to do with my attempts to somehow reach this place, where I can finally be at rest with Dad and myself. Much of what I fought for were my attempts to come to a reality where I could relax and know that the work was done. Yes, if truth were told, I heard about this supposed reality many times before. Many were the sermons and teachings I heard about Jesus saying on the cross that it was finished, or that Dad loved me and was proud of me. Yet the reality is that I didn't feel or experience it.

This lack of experience was mainly because I attempted to work it out within my mind. My aim was always to somehow reach a place where I could tangibly get a hold of it so that every time I fell into the waters of uncertainty, I could pull out a formula that would help me return to a space of peace and comfort. The reality, once again, is that I was not able to put such a formula together, nor was I able to fabricate a quick fix that would bring me back to that space of stillness and peace.

> We were found in Christ before we were ever lost in Adam. Christ's life was meant to open the way for us to return to what was already true about us.

This was not possible because what we are talking about here is something that, like many other things, the mind is just not able to figure out or understand. This is something we have to accept by faith and trust; even when we don't feel like it, it is still true and it is still very much the reality of who we really are at the core of our being.

Like many of us, I too have spent years praying the prayer where I have asked Dad to empty me of myself so I could be filled with Him—the notion that somehow we need to be obliterated so the Spirit of God can overtake us. Once again, the reality is that Dad does not desire this nor does He want to get rid of who we are. He made us and did so in His image and in His likeness. He did it out of love and He confirmed how pleased He was by calling it not just *good* when He was finished, but *very good*.

You and I—whether we are able to accept it or not—have to realize that God has made us one with Him. If we were not one with Him, none of us would be able to even take a breath of fresh air into our lungs, as Genesis 6:3 rightly tells us. The Bible is clear on this when it says that each of us lives, moves, and has our being in Him. (See Acts 17:28.) If this were conditional, then the Bible would say so, but it doesn't. The same goes for Jesus's words when He tells His disciples that He will be with them, and thus with us, until the end of time. Again, there are no conditions and no rules that have to be kept in order to make this a reality.

I am becoming more convinced each day that Dad's main objective is to help us discover this true Self of ours that was within Him even before the world began. We can see this clearly in Psalm 139:16, where the psalmist says, "Like an open book, you watched me grow from conception to birth; all the stages of my life were spread out before you, the days of my life all prepared before I'd even lived one day."

When we fully understand this Scripture, we become aware that if we were indeed in Him before the beginning of time, then it must mean that we were found in Christ before we were ever lost in Adam. Christ's life was meant to open the way for us to return to what was already true about us. This discovery is extremely important because at the same time we discover our true Self, we also discover who Dad truly is. This is what Jesus was referring to as the pearl of great price we would find in the field, and, when we found it, we would happily sell everything to buy that field. (See Matthew 13:45-46.) The great field is our life and the pearl is our true Self hidden within our heart. What that person then turns around and sells is his or her false self and everything that helped make that up, so they could then live their life from their true identity.

Have you found your pearl yet?

I know I hadn't found it and I wasn't even looking for it for most of my "Christian" walk, simply because I was never told this is what the whole thing is about. It is so obvious now that all of my public and private attempts for significance in the past have been great clues to show me how I was largely still operating out of my false self, where I saw myself separated from Dad. I was trying to create my own pearl, instead of discovering and reconnecting with the One who was already within me.

Jesus knew that when we discovered this pearl, we would also discover our Dad, and then our true Self would grow and be experienced in a similar and parallel fashion. Until we understand this, all we will try to do is discover God and try to hold on to our false self at the same time, which, as I have discovered the hard way, is just not possible. First John 4:20 is very clear on this when it says:

> If anyone boasts, "I love God," and goes right on hating his brother or sister, thinking nothing of it, he is a liar. If he won't love the person he can see, how can he love the God he can't see?

This fact has to be accepted by faith, and it is kept as a fact by something called grace. There is nothing we can do to make it more real, just like there is nothing we can do to make it less real. It is what it is because this is the way Dad designed it before the beginning of time. This reality needs to be accepted and embraced by faith, as we recognize that living in this dimension will represent us experiencing and seeing much mystery in our lives. This is why I believe Paul told us to "work out [our] salvation with fear and trembling" (Philippians 2:12 NASB).

The encouragement to work something out means we are being invited into a dimension where we will have to seek and search, and, as we remain present, we will discover truth that will help us work things out over time. Paul further emphasizes this mystery when he tells us we will experience fear and trembling while we do it. We do not fear and tremble when we are in the presence of something we know and can control. We only experience fear and trembling when we travel through spaces and places we do not know, understand, or have the ability to control.

Since I have started to loosen my grip around my false self and all my good ideas and theological arguments and have started to enter into the reality of my oneness with Dad, I have often felt a fear and trembling upon my false self. This is the same fear and trembling Paul must have felt on the road to Damascus and probably felt with every new revelation and discovery Dad showed him.

Is this how your walk with Dad feels like?

Gone are the days when I thought Dad watched my life develop from a distance until the day I raised my hand and prayed a prayer. The fact is that I understand He has been with me and within me ever since I breathed my first breath, like the modern hymn so accurately describes: "From life's first cry to final breath, Jesus commands my destiny. No pow'r of hell, no scheme of man, can ever pluck me from his hand."[1]

The truth is that He has walked with and watched over me every single day of my life. Not understanding this was possibly the main stumbling block toward not being able to recognize and accept that I am unconditionally loved in Christ. I always thought if He indeed watched me from a distance all those years and only joined me when I put my hand up, then that meant His love was conditional on me doing certain things. As I now know, this is not the case.

The minute we add any condition whatsoever to grace, it ceases to be grace. Perhaps there is another name for it, but it certainly isn't grace because grace cannot have any conditions attached to it. Again, this is just the way it is whether it appeals to us or not. Our oneness with Dad is not something we can fabricate, nor is it open to just a few lucky ones who are able to discover a secret formula along the way. This reality is open and true to every single one of us who have ever lived on this earth. No exceptions, no conditions.

I will never forget the first time I was able to capture this reality as I made a cup of tea. I pulled out a cup made out of clear glass from one of our cupboards in the kitchen. After the water boiled, I poured it into the cup and allowed the tea bag to steep for a few minutes. Once done, I grabbed the pot of sugar and put two teaspoons of sugar into it. As I began to stir, I could see the sugar going around in the tea until it disappeared. As I stood there, I began to realize Dad was trying to show me something I had not understood.

Where was the sugar? I could no longer see it, but I knew it was in there because I could taste it once I had taken a sip of the tea. Had the tea taken over the sugar or had the water swallowed it and made it disappear? The fact was that neither of these were true. What had just happened before my eyes was Dad showing me what He in us and we in Him looks like.

The sugar was still there, and it was very much part of the cup of tea I had just made; however, as I poured it into the cup and it dissolved, it had become one with the contents. I could not see it but boy, could I taste it. For this to happen it was not necessary to remove the tea nor was it necessary to get rid of the water. The sugar had become part of what was already within the cup, just like the tea had done with the water.

The water didn't need to work hard to make this happen, nor did it have to do something specific for it to work. The tea didn't have to do anything either, and neither did the sugar. They simply blended into one another and became one as they made up what we have come to know and understand as a cup of tea—albeit a sweet one! All that was required from the three was a willingness to allow the other to do what they were naturally designed to do. Furthermore, once these had become one, it would be impossible for me to separate them again. This is how our oneness with Dad looks like and works.

Clearly, I am too aware that many of us don't see it this way. For us, this reality looks more like when we put together oil and water in a container, and no matter how hard we shake them, they do not mix nor do they blend with each other. This erroneous understanding is what then leads us to pray prayers like having more of Him and less of me—like we rightly believe that the oil or the water, whichever one we choose to be, needs to be taken out in its entirety before the other ingredient can take the container over.

Dad does not wish to take us over, nor does He wish to possess us. This is because He has placed Himself in us and we exist within Him. If this were not the case, we could not live nor could we survive a day in our life. He is the One who keeps everything going. Remember how it took Him breathing His breath into Adam to cause him to come alive? This same breath is the one we depend on to keep going in this life of ours. Without Him we cannot live, nor can we function the way we were designed. Not understanding this will not prevent Dad from continuing to give us breath and life, because thankfully He is not conditional like we are. In fact, it is this thought—that we somehow are able to continue living without Him—that is responsible for keeping us working so hard, even after we pray a prayer that tells us that from that point on Jesus has entered our lives. This view is empowered by our egotistical and independent mind that sees all things in separation from each other.

Jesus said, "Therefore you are to be perfect, as your heavenly Father is perfect" (Matthew 5:48 NASB). When I first read this, I thought Jesus had hit it out of the cosmic park with this statement. It took me a while to understand the reality of what Jesus had just said. Today, however, I am able to understand and accept it because I have finally realized He was not talking about perfect behavior as much as He was talking about our true identity, which had been placed there by Dad when He made us.

This perfection is within us not because we have done something special to deserve it, but because the One who made us, who is perfect and whole, deposited His spiritual DNA in us, just like any parent deposits their DNA into the child they are responsible for fathering or mothering. It does not matter what the child does or does not do, this DNA will be with them for the rest of their life because without it they could not exist. This is true whether a child knows their parents or not, whether they acknowledge them as their parents, whether they believe they exist or not, or whether they have ever met them.

Jesus prayed that "they may all be one; even as You, Father, are in Me and I in You, that they also may be in Us" (John 17:21 NASB). What did Jesus mean by this prayer? If we look at it at face value, we are seeing someone asking so others will be able to see this reality in their lives and each other just as Jesus saw it in His own life.

"So, Pablo, what you are saying is that we are God," you may be thinking. No, what I am saying is that every time you see yourself in the mirror or you see someone else, you can see God in him or her because that person carries the spiritual DNA of God. This spiritual DNA is not separated from you, nor is it only a part of your being, but instead this DNA is blended together as one with the whole of your being. In fact, each one of us in our true Self is a different expression of Dad's personality and identity, and that's why I believe that DNA truly means Do Not Alter.

Unfortunately, the reason we can't see this is because we try to work it out with our dualistic minds that say this is either one or the other. This is what Jesus was saying to the Pharisees when He said to them, "You search the Scriptures because you think that in them you have eternal life; it is these that testify about Me" (John 5:39 NASB). It is impossible to understand this reality or even begin to live in the reality Jesus lived in from our dualistic mind or any study we may undertake. The only way we can understand, see, and live from this reality is from our heart.

In fact, one of the biggest clues that will help us see we are not living in this reality is when we make it our aim to always try to get it right. This approach shows us once again that we are seeking to please someone who is separated from us and is, therefore, demanding a certain level of accomplishment before they accept us. This is the kind of thinking we are overtaken by when we try to fulfill the law instead of accepting His grace. It is not the gospel Jesus shared with us. If there is one word that could be used to encapsulate the message of the gospel, it would have to be the word *return*, which is what Jesus was saying to us when He told us to repent.

In fact, what Jesus was saying all along is that we are to return to the reality of the Garden before Adam got lost; return to our heart where we will find our original true Self blended together with Dad's DNA; and return by looking at things from a place that is beyond our mind, as our mind is not designed like our heart to see who we really are. This again is exactly what Paul was pointing to when he told us about the need for our minds to be transformed.

I realize this is a hard pill to swallow, because this would mean that much of what we have done in the name of getting it right would appear a complete waste of time and has had the direct opposite effect. The truth is that the reasons why we did it were so we could receive all that we have been already freely given. But as I have understood in my own journey, it is necessary as it brings us to the end of our false self where we then have a chance to be able to loosen our grip from all of our trying.

I was snowed in at a close friend's house in Pennsylvania, which meant we could not do much apart from talk, sleep, surf the net, and watch TV. As we sat in our big American La-Z-Boy chairs, a program came on about a new super car Toyota was planning to make. The man responsible for the design was asked if there was one key trait that enables someone to develop such an amazing design. His answer is remarkably simple, yet it opens my eyes to understand what Jesus meant when He told us to be like little children. The man says that without a doubt, the key trait would have to be the ability to be able to be like a child again. He explains that when one is able to draw and design from that perspective, an individual is free and has no inner visions, nor are they boxed in by any sophisticated mental arguments that tell him or her what is possible and impossible. As I am listening to all of this, I remember the words of Jesus in Matthew 18:3: "I'm telling you, once and for all, that unless you return to square one and start over like children, you're not even going to get a look at the kingdom, let alone get in."

Children are able to accept things at face value, no matter what they look like or how sophisticated they are. I know if I tell any of my young kids anything, they will just believe me. They won't try to work it out, nor will they try to do something themselves to make what I said any more true. They will just accept it as the way it is and make it a part of their lives because they trust me and have faith in me. Children are able to see, unlike most grown-ups who have filled their life with filters of knowledge, which, like with the Pharisees, often get in the way of seeing. Jesus said the Kingdom of heaven was here and within us—not out there or somewhere else, but within our heart. If we don't just accept this, trying to figure it out will only add baggage to this reality, and it is this same baggage that prevents us from finding the narrow way Jesus spoke about.

Furthermore, Jesus unmasked the false notion that our humanity separates us from God by demonstrating that the two can be one. If our humanity was so repulsive and disgusting, then Jesus could never have been a human. Yet as we all know, He was 100 percent human. This is the same with our new hearts we are given. If they were as wicked and as deceitful as many tell us they are, then how could we begin to even fulfill the first commandment Jesus spoke about, which tells us to love the Lord our God with our whole heart?

Our new heart is more than capable of loving the Lord our God, as neither our humanity nor our heart are the repulsive things many of us believe and have been taught they are. The minute we realize this is the minute we can begin to live fully integrated lives where our humanity (body and mind), our heart, our soul, and our spirit can live and function together as one. Adam, before he got lost in the Garden of Eden, and Jesus lived this way, and we can too because we have everything Jesus and Adam had without exception within and without.

The minute that Dad's Spirit within me enabled me to finally understand this truth, the need to work hard to become something that would release the happiness and peace I looked so hard for completely disappeared. In its place surfaced the rest Jesus and the book of Hebrews spoke about, a rest to be who I was originally made to be.

My prayer is that as you have read this book, you will realize you were okay and there was nothing wrong with your true Self apart from you not being able to see this truth about who you truly are. This state of unconsciousness meant you behaved and did things that fell far short of who you really are. This is what Jesus came to show and save us from, and that is the illusion of separation that our false self leads us to believe and drives us to work so hard as we try to bridge that gap.

Dad never left us. Dad never turned His back on us. Dad never stopped loving us. Dad never watched us from a distance. Dad never betrayed us. Dad never gave up on us, nor was He ever separated from us. If He did, then He never would have spared Noah and his family, giving them a chance to start over. Are you able to believe this as a child would, without doing anything to make it any more real?

The cause of our imperfection is that we have been captured by the beliefs within our heads that are simply not true. These beliefs have been shared all over the world, and the majority of us hold on to them as truth. We do this as we see so many others believing the same things, so we assume that they must, therefore, be truth. Amazingly, we take no time to consider them or even challenge them.

This is the self-destructive narrative we all carry within us, an approach we choose to take in life that gives us the feeling that we are okay. In reality it only leads us to a place of isolation that affirms the false belief that we are all separated. We all express this approach in many ways, every day—with protective mechanisms we all carry to cover our hearts and lives. These are the prisons of insecurity and fear that lead us to create false identities so we manage to get others to like us. We need to understand that all of this will only prevent us from seeing our true Self.

Unfortunately, not many of us dare to step out of this broad path to take a closer look out of fear of what may or may not happen. I thank Dad that He enabled me to start this journey some years back. During this time, I have traveled through many valleys and dark places. It has not been easy to leave the shores of familiarity where everyone swims in the safety of the beach of tradition. It has meant having to lie down and shed much of what I believed about Dad, life, and myself. Yet, as I have done this, I have gone from a place of predictability and a false sense of security to a place where I have felt like an atheist at times.

Time and time again, as those false beliefs vacated the house, a void was left open. This meant I found myself traveling through these voids of emptiness and darkness as my false knowledge had been clearly wiped out with the false identity and beliefs. Thankfully, because I was willing to take the journey with Dad, my true Self, who was responsible for taking up the place that was once held by what was not true, was revealed to me.

Because of this, things like mystery and faith have suddenly become easier to accept as I realize now I have been made to live in these dimensions and not in the predictable I can control. Reading the Bible, praying, and doing anything else I used to do out of duty have become a joy to do when I have the opportunity. If I don't, it is still okay because I know I am perfect, not because of what I can do but because of whose DNA I carry.

The perfection Jesus spoke about is not something we work our way into and neither is it something that is put together over time. This perfection Jesus spoke about is something we accept and a reality we are led into. What takes time is discovering it, accepting it, and understanding what it looks like to live from it—this is why a journey of discovery is required.

I am hoping that throughout this book, I have given you some clues as to what that might look like by sharing from a vulnerable and honest place some of the dimensions we encounter when we choose to live from our heart. Jesus understood and saw things as they truly were. He saw that our perfection had nothing to do with what met the eye. He understood our problem and condition well, and that's why He died for us; but not before He shared some truths about us and life as a whole. By what He said, He showed all of us He understood our true identity was not that of a sinner and our true and original Self was not capable of sinning either. Romans 7 supports this when Paul says, "For apart from the Law sin is dead. I was once alive apart from the Law" (Romans 7:8-9 NASB).

Jesus didn't condemn us, and neither did He place false expectations on us, and that's why we must not do this with others. Instead, He invited us to take a break because He knew the answer would not be found in the yoke we carried while trying to get it right, but instead in that place of rest we would find within our heart where the reality of the Kingdom of heaven is.

He encouraged us to love one another and ourselves; He was able to see we are all connected and one in Him. And if we didn't love one another, but instead used and hurt others, then we would only be using and hurting ourselves. He described this well when He gave us the picture in John 15:5: "I am the vine, you are the branches; he who abides in Me and I in him, he bears much fruit, for apart from Me you can do nothing" (NASB). This beautiful picture is mentioned again in Ephesians 4:25: "In Christ's body we're all connected to each other, after all. When you lie to others, you end up lying to yourself."

This describes how all of us, although we are our own unique and individual person resembling something about Dad that no one else does, are nevertheless connected because we are all part of the same vine. Jesus said that disconnection from Him would mean that we are not able to live from our true Self, as we would, in essence, be disconnecting ourselves from our heart.

We see this again when Jesus says, "If anyone does not abide in Me, he is thrown away as a branch and dries up; and they gather them, and cast them into the fire and they are burned" (John 15:6 NASB). If we ever became disconnected from the vine, then we would not be able to function, nor would we be able to live. It is also clear from these two passages that Jesus is sharing that unless we live from our heart, we will be unable to bear any fruit in our lives—not successes or accomplishments, but fruit—fruit that brings indirect change to our behavior, lasts, and which others can feed on as they cross our paths.

The choice is ours. Are we going to persevere and walk under the illusion of separation, or are we going to allow our heart to be healed and awakened so we can indeed see that a reconnection to the reality within our heart is needed and delivered through Christ? In my life, as I have chosen to loosen my grip around my false self, this has slowly but surely been shed off and burned up.

John the Baptist says of Jesus at the beginning of his ministry:

I'm baptizing you here in the river, turning your old life in for a kingdom life. The real action comes next: The main character in this drama—compared to him I'm a mere stagehand—will ignite the kingdom life within you, a fire within you, the Holy Spirit within you, changing you from the inside out. He's going to clean house—make a clean sweep of your lives. He'll place everything true in its proper place before God; everything false he'll put out with the trash to be burned (Matthew 3:11-12).

I know many have said this burning up is speaking of hell. However, I believe that all hell means is a loss of divine union that in the present describes a state of consciousness that is unaware of the truth. So in other words, if we choose to allow our false self to be the main driver in our lives, then this will lead us to wrongly believe that we are indeed separated from our true source, which will mean it will be living hell.

The truth is that my life was hell, even after I had put my hand up all those many years ago, because I remained unconscious of the truth. Seeing this truth has meant I have been suddenly enabled to begin to function and feed my life no longer from the false self, but from the true one that was within me all along, but which I couldn't see. Becoming aware of this disconnection has meant that the true identity, purpose, meaning, love, joy, peace, happiness, acceptance, wisdom, understanding, health, hope, faith, value, worth, security, protection, grace, and peace I always longed for have begun to flow. I have been shown the way to "return" to the one and true vine who has been within my heart all along.

Ultimately, oneness is found throughout the Bible. From its first words we see a Trinity who, although distinct in their own expression, are one and the same. Then, as we take a look at the beginning, we see a great void. Not a void in the negative sense of the word—empty because of lack—but one that was full of the one reality that was the essence of God. What had not yet happened was for that essence to manifest Himself in form or substance. The form and substance began to take place from within Dad as He began to speak it into being. This eventually led to Adam being made in the image and likeness of Dad from the dust that made up what He had spoken into being from within Himself. Then came Eve, who was not made separate from Adam but, in fact, came from within him. From there, reproduction began to take place from this original seed as men and women became one flesh and reproduced.

Next, we look at Jesus and see Him speaking of oneness and wholeness, not just once but several times. He tells us if we see Him, we see the Father. He speaks of us being in Him and He in us. He speaks of being in the Father and the Father being in Him. He gives us advice that shows a connection between everything that exists when He tells us to love one another and do unto others what we would want them to do unto us. Later, Paul speaks about a body and how when even the smallest member is cut off, the body suffers because we are all joined together under the one head, Christ.

Have you ever wondered where your soul starts and ends? Where is the boundary where your heart and spirit meet? The truth is that you cannot and you will not ever know this, because we are a part of this wonderful reality of an invisible oneness. Furthermore, and most importantly, we are also told clearly that all of us are in Him and it is in Him that we live, move, and have our being. We need to understand that everything and everyone is within God and He is within them. This is because if anyone or anything is outside of God, then God can't be God.

Therefore, it is my hope that you are beginning to understand that the reality of all that I have shared with you throughout this book is what we have woken up to and will continue to wake up to every morning. Yes, the truth is that many of us have gone through entire days, and we will continue to do so, where our true Self is quietly and peacefully observing us from within because we keep focusing on improving and building our outer image, which has been responsible for blinding us from our true one. This is why so many of us often feel so lost, tired, isolated, and aimless, even if we pretend to be experiencing something different.

Today, my friend, you hold the decision in your hands as to how much longer you will continue to live like this and practice a faith that will be no more than a devotional habit instead of the transformational practice it was always meant to be. Only you can determine how much longer you will continue to find your image and identity in the attachments and preferences you have built around your false self. It is entirely up to you if you will continue to allow yourself to upset the course of your life every time these attachments and preferences are not met.

Remember, the true identity, purpose, meaning, love, joy, peace, happiness, acceptance, wisdom, understanding, health, hope, faith, value, worth, security, protection, grace, and peace that you need are already within you. There is nothing lacking. All that is lacking is you finally making the decision to listen and reconnect with your heart, and allowing the One who is fused together with you to show you the unforced rhythms of grace. I am certain that as you do this, you will be able to see your true Self, God, and your circumstances as they truly are because you will finally be living and seeing through the eyes of your resurrected true Self within your heart!

PRAYER

God—well, here I am at the end of this book. To be honest, I have seen and read so much I have never considered before. So much in me wants to no longer be robbed of all that You have put in me, God. I want to discover the pearl within my life because I now know that when I do this, I will be walking into the full reality of my oneness with You.

I want to be able to enjoy the sunset and intimate moments with loved ones. I want to enjoy everything that is around me as I go about my days. I want to live from this place of rest where I can work but not toil and force things to happen. I just want to enjoy this moment and say thank You for what You have done for me, and thank You for this opportunity I have been given to discover what this has always been about—to live and walk in the reality where I am one with You. I am excited about the future, not because of what I am going to become, but because of what I am going to discover about You and me. I love You, God. Amen.

POINT OF ACTION

Focus on one person you often see, and ask God to help you see His image and nature in that person. As time goes by and you practice this, let the same eyes that you see this person with be the ones you use to see others and yourself.

NOTE

1.   Keith Getty and Stuart Townend, writers, *In Christ Alone*, Kingsway Music Thankyou Music, 2001, CD.

ABOUT PABLO GIACOPELLI

Pablo Giacopelli has been involved in high-performance environments since an early age, first as a competitive player and later as a professional coach. He has had the opportunity to successfully coach some of the best female players in the world of tennis. He was selected to be the tennis team captain for Estonia in the 2008 Beijing Olympics. His pupils' successes have ranged from quarterfinal showings at Grand Slams to winning major WTA events to top-ten yearly rankings. He is a personal and professional performance coach certified by the Coach U Institute. He is also a certified professional performance tennis coach and has been trained in sports psychology. Pablo has traveled around the world several times and speaks four languages. He has been a guest speaker at various conferences and seminars around the world. Lately, Pablo has been coaching people from all walks of life to develop their personal and professional life and leadership potential through individual coaching and his very popular online course, under the banners of UXL and The Zone Project. During the course of 2015, Pablo is planning to relocate to the USA to expand the work with The Zone Project. Pablo is married to Madeleine and has been based in Tel Aviv, Israel for the last four years. He is the father of five children—Vanessa, Jake, Mia, Gisella, and Anabella.

To find out how Pablo expresses his work please visit:

www.thezoneproject.com

www.uxlinlife.com

www.holdingonloosely.com

To book Pablo for a speaking engagement please contact him directly at:

pablo@uxlinlife.com

OTHER BOOKS BY PABLO GIACOPELLI

Holding on Loosely